THE MARKETS OF ASIA/PACIFIC: PHILIPPINES

The Asia Pacific Centre is the London-based associate of the Survey Research Group. SRG consists of market research companies in Hong Kong, Singapore, Philippines, Malaysia, Indonesia, Thailand and Australia.

THE MARKETS OF ASIA/PACIFIC

THE PHILIPPINES

The Asia Pacific Centre

Facts On File, Inc.

460 Park Avenue South,
New York, N.Y. 10016

Copyright © by the Asia Pacific Centre Limited 1982.

Published in the United Kingdom in 1982 by Gower Publishing Company Limited, Croft Road, Aldershot, Hampshire GU11 3HR, England.

Published in the United States of America in 1982 by Facts on File, Inc., 460 Park Avenue South, New York, N.Y. 10016.

Library of Congress Cataloguing in Publication Data

Main entry under title:

The Markets of Asia/Pacific — Philippines

   Includes index.
   1. Philippines — Economic conditions — 1946-
   2. Philippines — Commerce.   I. Asia Pacific Centre.
   HC455.M37   330.9599'046   81-3238
   ISBN 0-87196-590-9   AACR2

Printed in Great Britain

Contents

List of Tables

Foreword

'THE MARKETS OF ASIA PACIFIC' SERIES

The series of books under the title 'The Markets of Asia Pacific' is designed to provide an overview of some of the fastest growing and most dynamic markets in the world. The series will be periodically updated; for most countries, every two years.

An important feature of the series is the release for the first time of the banks of market data owned by the Survey Research Group of Companies (SRG). SRG is the largest group of market research companies operating in the Asia Pacific region and heavy investment in syndicated research of their own has led to a considerable amount of new market research information becoming available. Almost all the SRG information published in this series cannot be found in any other published source.

Where SRG information exists, it has considerable depth but it covers by no means all the markets of interest. It has therefore been supplemented by key published statistics from elsewhere. The selection of published statistics has been derived from a search of existing data sources. While it is clearly beyond the scope of the series to quote from all sources found, a listing of titles and locations is included as an important feature in each country book.

In setting a style for the series, emphasis has been put on the provision of hard information rather than interpretative discussion. Wherever possible, however, key points of market development are described in the text. In effect, this is designed as a reference series which should provide mostly numeric answers to a range of marketing questions. To facilitate reference a detailed index is provided at the back of the book.

The broad format of each country book is similar but there is some variation in specific content. This is determined by the particular market characteristics of the country and the data that happens to be available.

PHILIPPINES

This volume draws heavily on surveys conducted by the Pulse Group of Companies* in the past 2 years. This is the first occasion on which most of this information has been released for general publication and it provides an overview of the main media and consumer markets. We acknowledge the data provided by Consumer, Dealer and Media Pulse and their help in identifying key market trends and characteristics.

Most of the other information in this book has been drawn from Government sources and from the reports of the Central Bank of the Philippines. Our use of statistics from these sources is gratefully acknowledged.

Individual sources are referenced in the appropriate chapter.

In producing this book our intention has been to provide hard statistical information across a range of markets and where possible to include information of our own.

We propose to update this volume on a two-yearly basis. For the interim, the statistics selected should provide the reader with at least a good indication of the main parameters of the markets. Where the latest figures are essential the reader is invited to refer to the Asia Pacific Centre Ltd. who will either provide them or indicate the best source.

* Member of the Survey Research Group

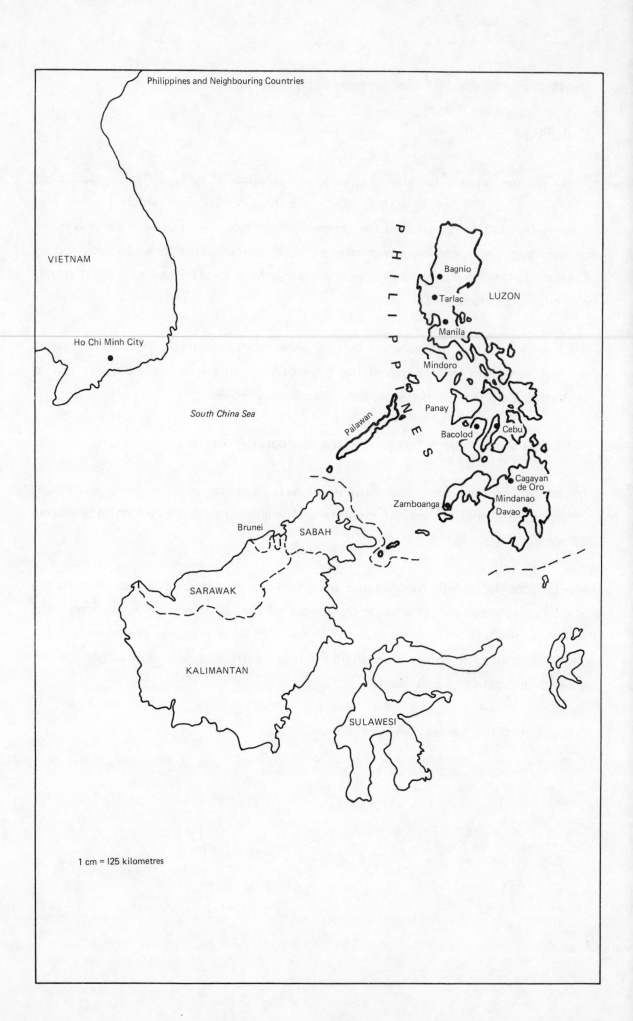

Philippines and Neighbouring Countries

VIETNAM

Ho Chi Minh City

South China Sea

PHILIPPINES

Bagnio

Tarlac

LUZON

Manila

Mindoro

Panay

Palawan

Bacolod

Cebu

Cagayan
de Oro

Zamboanga

Mindanao

Davao

Brunei

SABAH

SARAWAK

KALIMANTAN

SULAWESI

1 cm = 125 kilometres

1 Economic and Political Background

ECONOMIC BACKGROUND

Of all the non-communist countries in Southeast and East Asia, the Philippines has achieved the lowest economic growth rates throughout the last decade. It fell to 4%-5% in 1980, compared with 6%-8 in most of the other ASEAN countries, and the 10% average of Hong Kong.

The economy is heavily dependent on a small number of primary commodities, whose world prices fluctuate severely, notably coconut and sugar. The country has to import most of its energy, and the price increase for oil in 1974 caused a doubling of the import bill in that year. The result has been a widening trade deficit which reached US$1.9 billion in 1980. There are plans to develop alternative energy sources, particularly coal, geothermal and alcohol from sugar cane, but it will be some years before the effect of this will be reflected significantly in the economy.

Table 1 - GDP growth rate

	1975	1976	1977	1978	1979	1980
% annual growth	5.9	6.1	6.1	6.3	5.8	4.7

Source: National Economic and Development Authority

The Philippines was the first country in Southeast Asia to begin industrialisation, which started in 1950 with generous assistance from the US. It has not however been particularly successful, and the manufacturing share of GDP has stagnated at about 24% for the last five years. There has been a shortage of direct foreign investment, which is crucial in industrial development, as much for the importation of technology and management skills as for the money. Political uncertainty, both at a central level and a local industrial level, has been a major factor in this.

The government is making sustained efforts to remedy this situation, and a number of new laws and presidential decrees have been enacted in the last few years.

Table 2 – GDP by Industrial origin

	1970	1975	1977	1979
	%	%	%	%
Agriculture, fisheries and forestry	27.8	28.8	27.4	24.2
Industrial Sector	29.6	33.8	34.2	35.2
Mining & quarrying	2.8	1.8	1.7	2.6
Manufacturing	22.6	24.9	24.3	24.3
Construction	3.6	6.2	7.3	7.3
Electricity, gas & water	0.6	0.9	0.9	1.0
Service Sector	42.6	37.4	38.4	40.6
Transport, communication & storage	4.2	4.1	5.4	6.6
Commerce	24.8	22.1	21.9	23.3
Services	13.6	11.2	11.1	10.7

Source: National Economic and Development Authority

The major two primary commodities on which the Philippines has relied, and still does are coconuts and sugar. Unfortunately, not only do prices fluctuate on the world market, but the Philippines is dependent on a small number of importing countries. The government is pursuing an aggressive development and promotion policy for exports and diversification of markets is an important objective.

The export promotion programme has had a significant effect in increasing exports away from the traditional products, and despite the stagnation of industrial development, exports of manufactured items have increased substantially.

Table 3 –   Exports by category

(% of value)	1975 %	1979 %	1980+ %
Traditional	**79.2**	**55.9**	**53.9**
Coconut products	20.3	21.0	13.6
Sugar products	26.9	5.2	11.6
Forest products	11.3	10.5	7.2
Mineral products	11.2	12.3	14.2
Fruit & vegetables	5.4	4.9	4.9
Abaca products	1.0	0.5	0.5
Tobacco	1.5	0.7	0.5
Petroleum lubricants	1.6	0.8	1.4
Non-traditional manufacture and non-manufacture	**19.7**	**43.1**	**45.3**
Others	**1.1**	**1.0**	**0.8**

Source: National Economic Development Authority (+ Estimate)

Table 3 demonstrates the vulnerability of dependence on too few primary commodities. A drastic fall in the international sugar price reduced its export share of value from 26.9% in 1975 to 5.2% in 1979, but it rose again to 11.6% in 1980.

A serious problem in the Philippines is the increasing rate of inflation in the last two years which has reached annual rates of about 20%. This has not been accompanied by increases in wages, with the result that real incomes have dropped. Real incomes of unskilled labourers in 1980 were 52.5% of the 1972 level, compared with 63.2% among skilled labour.

Table 4 –   Consumer price indices (1972 = 100)

	1976	1977	1978	1979	1980	1981
All items	**182.3**	**200.4**	**215.0**	**249.2**	**292.2**	**319.3**
Food, alcoholic beverages and tobacco	178.5	195.6	207.9	239.0	271.8	297.9
Clothing	195.2	215.5	235.6	272.1	336.6	365.6
Housing & repair	181.2	205.2	225.0	256.5	300.4	334.6
Fuel, light & water	189.2	205.2	230.5	287.7	388.2	445.9
Services	175.4	196.9	214.1	258.5	326.3	346.0
Miscellaneous	210.3	223.7	238.4	275.3	326.4	345.8

Source: National Census and Statistics Office

(Note: Figures for 1976, 1977 and 1978 are annual averages, 1979 and 1980 are figures for June, 1981 for February)

The real income decline is even less among the higher socio-economic groups, thus increasing the disparity between rich and poor in the Philippines, which was already considered to be the widest in Asia. The implications in business and political terms are serious. On top of this, poverty and malnutrition remain endemic problems in the Philippines.

POLITICAL BACKGROUND

In all Asian countries political factors are of crucial importance, and in no case is this more important than in the Philippines. The political problems of the Philippines are possibly more severe than in neighbouring countries. It is not the intention of this book to attempt a detailed analysis nor to make forecasts, but three points of substance should be considered.

'Martial' law was declared in 1972, and re-presented as an 'emergency' law in 1981. There does seem to be greater stability under President Marcos's regime, but most observers question how long this will last as opposition becomes more vocal. It is relevant that prior to martial law the Philippines probably had the most open and uninhibited political environment in Asia, very much founded on the American style. The long term stability of government is something about which observers ask questions.

Aggravating the problems of central government and the economy is the continuing drain of fighting a war in the South, with no apparent solution in sight. The gravity of this war, its drain on resources and its hampering effect on the President are almost certainly more serious than is generally appreciated outside the Philippines.

The serious decline in real incomes, and the widening of an already large gap between rich and poor, town and village add fuel to this unstable situation. A major part of the population is classified as living in poverty, and the Philippines has one of the highest PCM (protein caloric malnutrition) rates in Asia, and it has increased in the last decade.

The political problems of the Philippines are not helped by the economic problems, and vice versa. However, it must be cautioned that whatever may be the economic and political difficulties of the country, there are many companies conducting successful businesses in the Philippines, and it is necessary to distinguish individual market prospects from the macro-economic.

Table 5 - Economic Indicators

	1975	1978	1979	1980
Gross National Product (Current prices, million pesos)	114,265	175,777	215,659	269,781
Agriculture, fishing, forestry production (million pesos)	32,996	47,126	52,582	NI
Industrial production (million pesos)	38,692	60,237	76,526	NI
Services production (million pesos)	42,915	69,328	87,911	NI
Total trade (US$ million)	5,754	6,157	10,743	13,351
Domestic Exports (US$ million)	2,294	3,425	4,601	5,725
Consumer Price Index (1972 = 100)	166.9	215.0	249.2	292.2
Average Earnings Index (1972 = 100)				
Salaried	135.7	186.5	227.5	NI
Wages	125.3	164.4	195.4	NI
Balance of payments (US$ million)	(1,241)	(1,127)	(570)	(380)

Source: National Economic Development Authority

Table 6 - Annual changes in real GNP/GDP growth (for selected countries (1976-79)

	1976	1977	1978	1979
Percentage growth in GNP/GDP				
- Total OECD	5.2	3.7	3.7	3.4
- USA	5.8	4.9	4.4	2.3
- Japan	6.0	5.4	5.9	6.0
- West Germany	5.6	2.6	3.5	4.4
- France	5.6	3.0	3.5	3.7
- United Kingdom	2.6	2.0	3.4	1.1
- ASEAN				
- Indonesia	6.9	7.4	7.2	4.9
- Malaysia	11.6	7.7	7.5	8.5
- **Philippines**	**6.1**	**6.1**	**6.3**	**5.8**
- Singapore	7.2	7.8	8.6	9.3
- Thailand	9.3	7.3	11.7	6.7
Other				
- Hong Kong	16.7	9.8	10.0	11.5
- South Korea	15.1	10.3	11.6	3.5
- Taiwan	11.5	8.5	12.8	8.0

Sources:- OECD

Official Country Reports

Central Bureau of Statistics, Indonesia

Ministry of Finance, Malaysia

Singapore 1980 Budget Report

National Economic and Social Development Board, Thailand

National Economic and Development Authority, Philippines

Table 7 –   Annual changes in consumer prices for selected countries

	1976	1977	1978	1979
Percentage change in prices				
- Total OECD	8.6	8.7	7.9	9.9
- USA	5.8	6.5	7.7	9.0
- Japan	9.3	8.1	3.8	3.3
- West Germany	4.5	3.9	2.6	4.3
- France	9.6	9.4	9.1	10.7
- United Kingdom	16.5	15.9	8.3	12.2
- ASEAN				
- Indonesia	19.8	11.0	8.6	24.4
- Malaysia	2.6	4.7	4.9	3.6
- **Philippines**	**9.2**	**9.9**	**7.3**	**16.5**
- Singapore	-1.9	3.2	4.8	4.0
- Thailand	4.2	7.2	8.0	15.0
- Other				
- HongKong	3.4	5.8	5.9	11.6
- South Korea	15.4	10.1	14.4	18.3
- Taiwan	2.5	7.0	5.8	10.3

Sources:- OECD

Official Country Reports

Ministry of Finance, Malaysia

Singapore 1980 Budget Report

Bangkok Bank

Hong Kong Census and Statistics Department

National Census and Statistics Office, Philippines

(Note: The four volumes of 'Markets of Asia Pacific' covering Indonesia, Malaysia, Singapore, Thailand give the following figures

	1976	1977	1978	1978
Philippines	6.2	7.9	7.6	18.8

They were incorrectly described in the secondary source from which they were taken as being for the Philippines. They actually refer to Metro Manila above.)

2 The People

The population of the Philippines is estimated to have reached 49 million by the beginning of 1981. The growth rate is currently one of the highest in the region, averaging 2.8% in the Seventies.

The birth rate is declining and there are active population control programmes, resulting in a growth rate which was probably lower at the end of the last decade than it was in 1970. At the same time improved medical facilities have raised life expectancy from 56.5 years in 1965 to 60.6 in 1973. It should be mentioned that the Philippines is the only Christian country in Asia, and the overwhelming majority of the population is Roman Catholic. Despite a powerful presence in Filipino life, this does not seem to have presented a problem for the population control programmes. The medium fertility projection of the Population Centre Foundation in Manila is that the population will reach 80 million by the year 2,000, which represents an increase of over 60% on the present level.

Table 8 - Population projection for the Philippines

(millions)	1980	1985	1990	1995	2000
High	48	57	65	75	84
Medium	48	56	64	72	80
Low	48	54	59	64	68

Source: Population Centre Foundation

The average number of children per married couple is just over two in order to replace the population, but in the Philippines it is just under four, nearly double the number needed for replacement. It also has to be assumed that in the next two decades improvements in health care, and a reduction in malnutrition will increase life-expectancy.

GEOGRAPHICAL DISTRIBUTION

The Philippines is an archipelago of approximately 7,100 islands, many of which are uninhabited. The country is divided into 12 geographical regions, which are commonly used to analyse and present most national statistical data.

Table 9 – Population by geographic region (1981)

	Region No			
North	1	Ilocos	3.7	million
	2	Cagayan Valley	2.3	
	3	Central Luzon	5.0	
Central	4	Southern Tagalog	12.6	
	5	Bicol	3.6	
	6	Western Visayas	4.9	
	7	Central Visayas	3.9	
	8	Eastern Visayas	2.9	
South	9	Western Mindanao	2.5	
	10	Northern Mindanao	2.8	
	11	Southern Mindanao	3.4	
	12	Central Mindanao	2.3	

Source: National Census and Statistics Office

Southern Tagalog, overwhelmingly the most populous region contains Metro Manila, which accounts for half the population of the region, and which has grown substantially in recent years.

The Philippines is a relatively urbanised country, when compared with large ASEAN neighbours such as Indonesia and Thailand, and the degree of urbanisation is increasing. The proportion living in urban areas was 31.6% in 1979, nearly double the urban population of Thailand.

There is a strict definition in general application for the term 'urban', with criteria of population density, street pattern, commercial activity, public buildings, and in the smaller barrios occupation of the inhabitants.

In addition to Metro Manila, there are two cities of approximately ½ million inhabitants, and three with about ¼ million. In total there are exactly 100 towns with over 10,000 inhabitants spread throughout the Philippines.

Table 10 - Urban distribution by town size (1980)

	Population in '000s
Metro Manila	6,203
Davao	596
Cebu	478
Zamboanga	311
Bacolod	257
Iloilo	248
Basilan	207
Olongapo	201
20 towns	100-200
43 towns	50-100
20 towns	25-50
9 towns	10-25

Source: National Census and Statistics Office

ETHNIC GROUPS

The indigenous ethnic diversity of the Philippines distinguishes it from all of its neighbours except Indonesia. Peninsular Malaysia has a number of different race groups, but caused primarily by immigration. In the Philippines there are over 50 different ethnic groups, speaking nearly 100 dialects and languages. In recent years a previously unknown stone-age race was found in one of the remote islands of the archipelago.

There are 9 main languages, but in some provinces combinations of the main linguistic streams could expand that number. Within these main groups are the many dialects, totalling nearly 100. The main languages are:

Tagalog

Ilocano

Ifuago

Pampango

Ilonggo

Bicol

Cebuano

Waray-Waray

Tausog

Tagalog is the main language of the most important island in the Philippines, Luzon, and is the basic constituent of the national language Pilipino. English and Spanish are also official languages.

In addition to the immense indigenous diversity of the country the population has mixed freely with several other races, principally Spanish, American and Chinese. In Manila a group of Filipinos meeting together could look as if it were a group of people from several different races - Tagalog, Spanish, Mestiza, Chinese - but all would be Filipino, and in every way the same in behaviour and life-style. The Philippines therefore has one of the most complex mixtures of indigenous and immigrant races in the world.

The half century during which America occupied the Philippines has lead to one of the most extraordinary facts about the country: it contains the third largest English-speaking population in the world, after the USA and the UK. This should not however mislead the observer into perceiving the lifestyle as American rather than Filipino. Underneath this, Filipinos live a Filipino lifestyle, think as Filipinos, and at the grass roots level in the rural areas of the country life remains largely undisturbed by these cultural importations.

This is important for marketing organisations, or any institution seeking to communicate with or advertise to the population. Without a proper understanding of the linguistic diversity of the Philippines, and a feel for the Filipino way of life, it would be easy to make quite erroneous conceptual assumptions.

DEMOGRAPHIC PATTERNS

As would be expected from the high growth rate, 53% of the population is aged under 20, and 30% under 15.

Table 11 - Population profile by age and sex (1981)

	Total Philippines	
	'000s	%
Men	25,214	50.5
Women	24,666	49.5
0- 9	14,166	28.4
10-19	12,127	24.3
20-29	9,093	18.2
30-39	5,474	11.0
40-49	3,974	8.0
50-59	2,617	5.2
60+	2,429	4.9

Source: National Census and Statistics Office

The comparison of occupation analysis from data provided by Consumer Pulse, which is the most regularly up-dated information available in the Philippines, shows a steady decline in the proportion of people engaged in agricultural activities, and a corresponding increase in the number of craftsmen, skilled and unskilled workers and persons employed in the sales and service industries.

The increase in workers in the service industries is of some concern. Although an increased contribution to employment is desirable in the Philippines today, it would be preferable if it came from the manufacturing industries. This is not immediately likely however, given the stagnation of the manufacturing sector.

Table 12 – Occupation of head of household; 1975 and 1979 by urban/rural

	Total Philippines		Urban		Rural	
	1975	1979	1975	1979	1975	1979
	%	%	%	%	%	%
Professional, technical	5	5	11	10	2	2
Farmers	47	39	4	5	67	55
Managers, officials, proprietors	3	2	8	4	1	*
Clerical	4	3	9	8	1	1
Sales	7	9	12	16	4	5
Craftsmen, foremen	10	16	16	21	7	14
Service workers, except household	13	20	25	27	8	17
Household workers	1	1	2	1	1	1
Labourers	5	3	6	3	4	3
Not employed	6	3	9	5	4	2
Refused	1	1	1	1	*	1

Source: Consumer Pulse National Surveys

Across the Philippines 87% of the population are literate, the same for both men and women. There is some variation by region, and it is noticeable that in the five provinces with lower literacy levels, women are slightly less literate than men. Throughout the rest of the country literacy ranges from 79% (in Lanao del Norte, Occidental Mindoro, Sultan Kudarat, Zamboanga del Norte) to highs of 100% (in Batanes) and 99% (in Bataan, Camarines Norte and Camarines Sur).

The five provinces with lower literacy are Basilan (with 51%), Lanoa de Sur (46%) Maguindanao (49%), Sulu (51%) in the South; Ifuago (67%) and Mountain Province (71%) in the North. Literacy is lowest in the isolated provinces in the Southern Muslim region.

This drift away from agricultural occupations has been accompanied by increased educational levels in the rural Philippines.

Table 13 - Educational level of head of household; 1975 and 1979 by urban/rural

	Total Philippines		Urban		Rural	
	1975	1979	1975	1979	1975	1979
	%	%	%	%	%	%
No schooling	6	4	1	1	9	5
Some elementary	31	24	11	9	41	32
Completed elementary	22	24	15	15	25	29
Some high school	13	13	14	14	12	13
Completed high school	11	15	18	20	7	12
Some college	7	9	16	16	3	5
Bachelor's degree	9	10	23	23	3	4
Completed/some master's degree	1	1	1	1	*	*

Source: Consumer Pulse National Surveys

It is interesting that despite the influx of people into urban areas, particularly Manila, during the last few years, educational levels have been maintained at the same position.

With the exception of some isolated provinces in the far north and the south, education levels vary little across the Philippines, as would be expected from the literacy pattern described in the paragraphs before Table 13. It must be remembered that despite the high incidence of understanding English, 'literacy' means literacy in any language.

The figures in this table point to an important aspect of the Philippines, which has far-reaching implications for marketing organisations, and this is the extraordinarily wide coverage of the educational system, at all levels. In 1979 10% of all heads of household had a college or university degree of some sort. This rises to nearly a quarter in the urban areas, and 29% in Manila.

The following table compares educational enrolment at various points in the Seventies, in several countries.

Table 14 - Enrolment in educational institutions in selected countries

	Philippines	Thailand	UK	USA	Japan
Population (in millions)	42	42	55	215	112
Enrolment at:					
Pre-primary	53	215	50	4,858	2,292
1st level	8,365	6,686	5,386	26,848	10,365
2nd level	2,255	965	4,230	20,546	9,125
3rd level	765	78	547	11,185	2,249
(in '000s)					
Total% enrolment	27	19	19	30	24
	1975	1975	1973	1975	1975

Sources: Philippine Ministry of Education and Culture
World Bank
National Statistical Office of Thailand
Bureau of Statistics, Office of the Prime Minister, Japan

It is not meaningful to compare individual levels since there is wide variation by definition and quality from country to country. But the Philippines clearly has a wide educational franchise, wider than that of European countries and nearly as wide as that in the USA. It is of course wide, partly because education is improving rapidly, and with 53% of the population aged under 20, education levels therefore rise disproportionately faster than population. The number of college enrolments rose from 601,835 in 1971 to 1.1 million in 1979, and the number of public and private colleges from 634 in 1971 to 924 in 1975.

There are implications effecting both labour supply and marketing, caused by this wide educational system.

Firstly, a business organisation in the Philippines can draw on a supply of clerical labour with the highest standard of written English in South East Asia; even higher than in Malaysia and Singapore, both of which have a long English speaking tradition. For businesses which require a high standard of presentation this is a significant asset. A further aspect is the prevalence of academically trained and qualified people, to the extent that fairly low level jobs will be filled with people with professional qualifications. For example, in an accountancy office or department it is not unlikely that every clerk would have a college degree, or be a qualified accountant. This does not of course guarantee the standard.

Secondly, there are obvious marketing implications, in selling to and advertising to a target market with this wide education.

The average household income in Manila is approximately four times that of the average rural family, and about twice as high as that of the average family in towns outside Manila. Approximately half the rural houses in the country have earnings under £20 a month, compared with about 2% of homes in Manila.

3 Private Households

HOUSEHOLD CHARACTERISTICS

In 1979 there were estimated to be just under 8.2 million households in the
Philippines, with an average of 5.77 persons per household. The total number of
households grew from 7.2 million in 1975, but the average size decreased from
5.94.

Table 15 - **Number of private households and average number of persons
per household; 1975 and 1979 by urban/rural**

	Total Philippines		Urban		Rural	
	1975	1979	1975	1979	1975	1979
	%	%	%	%	%	%
Number of households ('000s)	7,208	8,192	1,152	1,479	4,958	5,710
Average number of persons per household	5.94	5.77	6.15	6.03	5.85	5.66

Source: National Census and Statistics Office

It was estimated that in 1977 there was a shortfall of 981,000 houses needed to
house the population. The 10-year Development Plan estimates a further
short-fall of 884,000 in the years 1980-87, totalling 1,865,000. The Government
has targetted to build over the next years, but in 1980 only achieved 54% of the
targetted 79,492 new houses.

In common with other countries with a large rural, agricultural population home
ownership is substantially higher outside the towns, although there has been an
increase in urban home ownership in the last few years.

Table 16 - Home ownership; 1975 and 1979 by urban/rural

	Total Philippines		Urban		Rural	
	1975	1979	1975	1979	1975	1979
	%	%	%	%	%	%
Own house	78	78	50	54	91	89
Rent house	15	13	44	35	2	3
Neither rent or own	7	9	7	10	7	8

Source: Consumer Pulse National Surveys

The most common materials of construction are aluminium or galvanised iron in urban areas (69% of urban houses), followed by nipa (25%). In the rural areas 66% of homes are made of nipa or cogon. It is, of course, the fragility of this material which contributes to the high requirement for new homes, aggravated by the annual typhoon problem in the Philippines.

Rapid strides have been made in the provision of electric power for domestic use. Although the information is not strictly comparable, the 1970 Census measured 23% of homes in the Philippines using electricity for lighting. The Consumer Pulse figures in the following table show something like an increase of 10% of all homes each five years, and mainly in the provision of electric power in rural areas.

As will be seen in Chapter 5 there has not yet been a corresponding growth in ownership of consumer durables and equipment using the electricity supply.

Electricity, running water

Table 17 - Ownership of utilities; 1975 and 1979 by urban/rural

	Total		Urban		Rural	
	%	%	%	%	%	%
Households with						
- Electricity	33	44	84	85	9	25
- Running Water	20	19	55	48	4	5

Source: Consumer Pulse National Surveys

The provision of running water for domestic use does not show the same success. The 1970 Census of dwelling units showed a figure of 24%, which is consistent with the Consumer Pulse Survey of households showing a slightly lower figure five years later.   This suggests that the government has not matched the rapid population growth, in providing domestic utilities.   This is, suggested by the declining incidence of having piped water among DE households in the urban areas, where the urban population growth has been most marked.   In such conditions a drop in electricity usage would not be so likely, since it would be far easier to tap into the nearest supply.

Electricity, running water

**Table 18 – Ownership of utilities; 1975 and 1979 by socio-economic class
(Total urban Philippines)**

	AB		C		D		E	
	1975	1979	1975	1979	1975	1979	1975	1979
	%	%	%	%	%	%	%	%
Household with								
- Electricity	100	99	99	99	89	91	61	58
- Running Water	100	99	91	88	53	47	18	12

Source: Consumer Pulse National Surveys

The median household size is about 5 members both in urban and rural figures, and the average is slightly higher.   It is interesting to note that only 5% of all households in the Philippines have as few as two or even one member.

Table 19 – Size of household; 1975 and 1979 by urban/rural

	Total Philippines		Urban		Rural	
	1975	1979	1975	1979	1975	1979
	%	%	%	%	%	%
Size of household:						
2 or less	6	5	5	5	6	5
3	10	11	11	10	10	12
4	16	14	17	15	15	14
5	17	17	16	17	17	17
6	14	16	15	15	14	16
7	13	12	12	12	14	12
8	8	10	8	9	8	10
9	7	7	6	6	7	7
10	4	4	4	4	4	4
11	2	2	2	2	2	2
12 or more	2	3	3	4	1	2

Source: Consumer Pulse National Surveys

HOUSEHOLD INCOME AND EXPENDITURE PATTERNS

The following tables are extracted from regular quarterly sample surveys conducted nationally by Consumer Pulse, and analyse claimed monthly household earnings. It shows a ratio of approximately 4:2:1 in the average earnings of families in Metro Manila: other urban: rural areas. During the period incomes have risen nationally by 25% in cash values.

Table 20 - Monthly household income; 1975 and 1979 by urban/rural

	Total Philippines		Urban		Rural	
	1975	1979	1975	1979	1975	1079
	%	%	%	%	%	%
Monthly income:						
200 or less (pesos)	29	21	5	4	41	19
201 - 300	22	16	13	7	26	20
301 - 400	14	11	15	10	13	12
401 - 600	13	14	19	18	10	12
601 - 800	6	7	12	12	3	5
801 - 1,000	4	5	9	10	1	3
1,001 - 2,000	5	6	12	16	1	2
2,001 or more	3	5	8	12	*	2
Not known/Refused	6	14	8	11	5	15

Source: Consumer Pulse National Surveys

Table 21 - Monthly household income in urban areas by socio-economic class (1979)

	AB	C	D	E
	%	%	%	%
Monthly income:				
200 or less (pesos)	--	--	2	15
201 - 300	--	*	5	20
301 - 400	*	1	9	20
401 - 600	*	3	22	23
601 - 800	1	5	17	9
801 - 1,000	1	9	14	4
1,001 - 2,000	8	31	18	2
2,001 or more	69	34	5	*
Not known/Refused	21	16	10	7

Source: Consumer Pulse National Surveys

However, while incomes have risen, so has the consumer price index, and at the end of 1979 it stood at 160 on a 1975 base of 100. The net result of this is that over the five years 1975-1979 average earnings have dropped by about 22% in terms of consumer purchasing power.

Table 22 – Consumer Price Index (Philippines)

		1972 = 100	1975 = 100
(Average)	1975	167	100
	1976	182	109
	1977	200	120
	1978	215	129
	1979	254	152
	1980	296	177
	1981 (Feb)	319	191

Source: National Economic and Development Authority

Average cash incomes in rural areas have held up well compared with the national average and particularly compared with urban areas outside Manila.

Table 23 – Average household income increases; Manila/urban/rural

	(1975 = 100)			
	Metro Manila	Other Urban	Rural	Total Philippines
1979 Average household income (pesos)	135	118	141	125

Source: Consumer Pulse National Surveys

Nevertheless this should not obscure the fact that in 1979 nearly one half of all rural homes in the Philippines had a monthly cash income of less than sterling £20, compared with one in ten urban homes.

The distribution of household expenditure shows a comparable pattern in urban and rural areas, but in the rural homes a higher proportion of (the lower level of) earnings is spent on the major single category 'food, beverages, tobacco'. The following table is from the 1975 Household Expenditure Survey, but the percentages can broadly be applied to more recent income data, and inserted at the top are the 1979 Consumer Pulse income averages. The percentages hardly varied through the four Household Expenditure Surveys conducted by National Census and Statistics Office in 1961, 1965, 1971 and 1975.

Table 24 – Household income and expenditure; Manila/urban/rural

	Metro Manila	Other Urban	Rural
Average monthly household income 1979	Pesos 1,465	Pesos 784	Pesos 375
Household expenditure 1975	%	%	%
Food, beverages and tobacco	49.4	50.7	61.4
Clothing, footwear and other wear	7.7	7.4	7.5
Housing	13.1	11.5	6.5
Household furnishing and equipment	1.8	2.1	1.7
Household operations	1.8	2.2	2.0
Fuel, light and water	4.7	4.7	4.5
Personal care	2.1	2.1	1.6
Medical care	1.7	2.0	1.8
Transport and communication	4.8	4.3	2.8
Recreation	1.8	1.8	1.2
Education	4.4	4.8	3.5
Gifts, contribution and assistance to outsiders	0.4	0.4	0.4
Taxes paid	1.8	1.2	0.9
Special occasions of family	1.3	1.7	2.1
Personal effects	1.4	1.1	0.9
Miscellaneous goods and services	2.0	2.0	1.2

Sources: Consumer Pulse National Surveys

National Census and Statistics Department

4 Consumer Markets – Non Durables

In this and the following chapters the objective is to provide a brief summary of some of the main consumer markets. For each market covered, size is given in terms of the number of consumers of the product, together with an indication of the leading brands. The leading brands are listed in order of their market share - again in terms of numbers of consumers.

The data in this chapter is all as recent as 1980, except for one table dealing with fruit flavoured drinks. Different tables are compiled from different rounds of the quarterly Pulse Urban Market Study, and thus have a high degree of comparability.

A basic feature of the consumer market in the Philippines is the extent to which it is influenced by American styles and methods and the length of time that major American consumer marketing companies have been established there. It is the only country in Southeast Asia in which Colgate, Unilever and Proctor and Gamble are all strongly established. Many other multi-nationals such as Johnson & Johnson, Richardson-Merril, SC Johnson have also been established there for many years. There are many Philippine-based companies manufacturing products and promoting them aggressively, often with marketing staff trained in these US multi-nationals.

There is a large disparity between spending power in urban and rural areas of the Philippines, and many companies tended to channel their marketing effort towards urban consumers. Many products thus have near saturation in urban areas, but low penetration rurally. Many organisations are now looking to the rural population for increased consumer offtake.

As everywhere in Southeast Asia, the Philippine market is complex, and the consumer unique. For example, the ethnic and linguistic diversity of the population is greater than in any other neighbouring country except Indonesia, but across this is overlaid the third largest English-speaking population in the world.

The implications for advertising, media planning and packaging are obviously complex.

Analgesics

Table 25 - Market summary by socio-economic class (urban 15+)

	Total	AB	C	D	E
'000s	7,212	433	1,298	3,894	1,587
	%	%	%	%	%
Have ever taken an analgesic	95	95	95	94	94

Leading brands:- Medicol, Biogesic, Neozep, Tylenol, Cortal.

Source:- Pulse Urban Market Study 1980

Market comment:- This product market is heavily fragmented by a large number of brands, although the top three brands have a total past month usage of approximately 80%.

The highest frequency consumers are older people, particularly women.

The market is dominated by tablets.

Canned Meat

Table 26 - Market summary by socio-economic class (urban 15+)

	Total	AB	C	D	E
'000s	7,212	433	1,298	3,894	1,587
	%	%	%	%	%
Ever use canned meat	78	86	87	70	63

Leading brand:- Purefoods

Source:- Pulse Urban Market Study 1980

Market comment:- This product market shows a strong American influence, with many American type products and terms in common use, as well as brands: franks, liverspread, Viennas or Wieners.

Frozen food displays in supermarkets also demonstrate the same influences with packaged meat products.

Fruit Flavoured Drinks

Table 27 - Market summary by socio-economic class (urban 15+)

	Total	AB	C	D	E
'000s	7,212	4,33	1,298	3,894	1,587
	%	%	%	%	%
Ever consumed a fruit flavoured drink	92	98	98	92	82

Leading brands:- Del Monte (juice), Tang (powder)

Source:- Pulse Urban Market Study 1979

Market comment:- The market is divided into three roughly the same sized segments, powder concentrate, liquid concentrate and fruit juice, with the last being slightly dominant.

Consumption is almost three times more frequent among ABs than among the lowest group, Es. This is particularly the case for the concentrates.

Jeans

Table 28 – Market summary by socio-economic class (urban 15+)

	Total	AB	C	D	E
'000s	7,212	433	1,298	3,894	1,587
	%	%	%	%	%
Own a pair of jeans	63	50	80	64	55

Leading brands:- Levi, Wrangler, Wynner

Source:- Pulse Urban Market Study 1980

Market comment:-   This is a highly fragmented market, with well over thirty brands.   The three market leaders account for two thirds of the consumers. Evidence of owning jeans peaks in the middle socio-economic range.

Floor Wax

Table 29 – Market summary by socio-economic class (urban 15+)

	Total	AB	C	D	E
'000s	7,212	433	1,298	3,894	1,587
	%	%	%	%	%
Ever use floor wax	91	98	94	95	77

Leading brands:- Johnson's, Yeo

Source:- Pulse Urban Market Study 1980

Market comment:-   This is a high penetration product market, overwhelmingly dominated by the leading brand, which is the regular brand for two-thirds of the consumers.

Usage in the lowest socio-economic groups is high in comparison with other countries in the region.

Insecticide

Table 30 - Market summary of socio-economic class (urban 15+)

	Total	AB	C	D	E
'000s	7,212	433	1,298	3,894	1,587
	%	%	%	%	%
Ever use insecticide	79	96	94	82	59

Leading brands:- Nuvan (liquid), Shelltox (liquid), Baygon (liquid)

Source:- Pulse Urban Market Study 1980

Market comment:- A high penetration product in the middle and upper socio-economic groups, there is lower usage in rural areas and urban Es. The market is still heavily dominated by liquid spray insecticide.

Toilet Soap

Table 31 - Market summary by socio-economic class (urban 15+)

	Total	AB	C	D	D
'000s	7,212	433	1,298	3,894	1,587
	%	%	%	%	%
Ever use toilet soap	92	94	93	94	89

Leading brands:- Lifebuoy, Safeguard, Palmolive, Irish Spring, Camay

Source:- Pulse Urban Market Study 1980

Market comment:- The leading brands are strong, but none has a consumer share in excess of 15%.

Talcum Powder

Table 32 - Market summary by socio-economic class (urban 15+)

	Total	AB	C	D	E
'000s	7,212	433	1,298	3,894	1,587
	%	%	%	%	%
Ever use talcum powder	99	99	99	99	99

Leading brands: Johnson's, Tender Care

Source:- Pulse Urban Market Study 1980

Market comment:- This very wide penetration market is heavily dominated by the leading brand, which has over half the consumer share, in a wide range of sizes and packs.

Deodorant

Table 33 - Market summary by socio-economic class (urban 15+)

	Total	AB	C	D	E
'000s	7,212	433	1,298	3,894	1,587
	%	%	%	%	%
Ever use deodorant	44	51	55	45	34

Leading brands:- Veto, Mum

Source:- Pulse Urban Market Study 1980

Market comment:- Although there is a fairly large difference between usage in the upper and lower class groups, 34% ever used in the Es is an extremly high figure compared with levels of usage in other countries in the region.

Cleansing Cream

Table 34 - Market summary by sex (urban 15+)

	Total	Male	Female
'000s	7,212	3,646	3,566
	%	%	%
Used cleansing cream in past 4 weeks	19	4	35

Leading brand:- Ponds

Source:- Pulse Urban Market Study 1980

Market comment:- The market is dominated by Ponds, which is the regular brand of over half the product users.

Skin/Hand/Body Lotion

Table 35 - Market summary by sex (urban 15+)

	Total	Male	Female
'000s	7,212	3,646	3,566
	%	%	%
Used lotion in past 4 weeks	42	26	59

Leading brands:- Johnson's, Jergens, Beautifont

Source:- Pulse Urban Market Study 1980

Market comment:- Although the level of usage is much higher by women, it is interestingly high among men.

Baby Oil

Table 36 – Market summary by socio-economic class (urban 15+)

	Total	AB	C	D	E
Houses with a baby	%	%	%	%	%
Ever use baby oil	93	97	95	94	90

Leading brand:- Johnson's

Source:- Pulse Urban Market Study 1980

Market comment:-   The leading brand dominates the market overwhelmingly. Usage has a high frequency in homes where the product is used.

In the last two years this product field has been widened to adult usage, following the 'New uses/New users' strategy launched in the US to expand a market at saturation point. It is being promoted for adult skin care, and as make-up remover.

The figures in Table 35 show that there is ample room for increased penetration of this market.

Baby Cologne/Freshener

Table 37 – Market summary by sex (urban 15+)

	Total	Male	Female
'000s	7,212	3,646	3,566
	%	%	%
Used baby cologne in past 4 weeks	50	41	59

Leading brand - Lord Wally

Source:- Pulse Urban Market Study 1980

Market comment:- This is a highly fragmented market, the leader being the only brand with as much as 5% consumer share.

There are also attempts for the product to be spread into adult usage, as is the case for other baby products.

Shampoo

Table 38 – Market summary by socio-economic class (urban 15+)

	Total	AB	C	D	E
'000s	7,212	433	1,298	3,894	1,587
	%	%	%	%	%
Ever use shampoo	94	97	96	95	89

Leading brands:- Palmolive, Prell

Source:- Pulse Urban Market Study 1980

Market comment:- The market is overwhelmingly dominated by liquid, and small use of powder or cream shampoo exists.

There is a very large number of brands competing for small shares of the market, but the two leaders between them have over a third consumer share of the market.

The market has doubled in the last two to three years, following the lead given by Palmolive in promoting sales in rural areas in very small quantities, on the 'tenggi' principle. Containers are opened in the retail outlet, consumers buy a small quantity for one occasion of use, and take it home in their own container, sometimes already half full of water.

Creme Rinse

Table 39 - Market summary by sex (urban 15+)

	Total	Male	Female
'000s	7,212	3,646	3,566
	%	%	%
Used creme rinse in past 4 weeks	12	9	16

Leading brands:- Gee, Revlon, Wella

Source:- Pulse Urban Market Study 1980

Market comment:- This small market is dominated by up-market brands.

Hair Spray

Table 40 - Market summary by sex (urban 15+)

	Total	Male	Female
'000s	7,212	3,646	3,566
	%	%	%
Used hairspray in past 4 weeks	2	*	5

Source:- Pulse Urban Market Study 1980

Market comment:- A very low penetration product, with much room for expansion.

Men's Hairdressing/Pomade

Table 41 – Market summary by sex (urban 15+)

	Total	Male	Female
'000s	7,212	3,646	3,566
	%	%	%
Used men's hairdressing in past 4 weeks	24	39	9

Leading brands:- Tancho, 3 Flowers, Palmolive

Source:- Pulse Urban Market Study 1980

Market comment:- This is one of the few consumer non-durable product fields in the Philippines where a Japanese brand has established itself in the leading position against the strongly established American brands.

5 Consumer Markets – Durables

The data from Consumer Pulse about the penetration of consumer durables in the Philippines adds a further dimension to knowledge of the country, because it is also available for the rural as well as urban areas. It tells a story which is similar to those of the other large countries in the region; the enormous difference in wealth between the urban and rural populations.

Approximately two thirds of the homes in the Philippines possess a radio, and there has been a steady increase throughout recent years. The penetration in rural areas has been growing faster than in urban areas.

Radio

Table 42 – Ownership of consumer durables 1975 and 1979 by urban/rural

	Total		Urban		Rural	
	1975	1979	1975	1979	1975	1979
	%	%	%	%	%	%
Households with a radio	60	67	72	77	54	63
Transistor	50	56	46	53	52	56
Power	4	12	10	26	1	6
FM band	5	13	15	31	1	4

Source: Consumer Pulse National Surveys

Comparison between the next and previous tables demonstrates another important socio-economic condition. The penetration of radio in urban E class homes is lower than in rural homes, 56% versus 63%, although it is increasing at a similar rate. This is very largely due to the influx of unskilled labourers into the urban areas, especially Manila and the large cities.

Radio

Table 43 - Ownership of consumer durables
1975 and 1979 by socio-economic class
(Total urban Philippines)

	AB		C		D		E	
	1975	1979	1975	1979	1975	1979	1975	1979
	%	%	%	%	%	%	%	%
Household with a
Radio	96	99	89	94	74	79	48	56
Transistor	28	74	44	58	52	49	42	44
Power	18	64	21	45	16	25	6	8
FM band	62	89	36	67	8	25	1	5

Source: Consumer Pulse National Surveys

It is also interesting that although 44% of homes in the Philippines are recorded as having electricity only 12% use a power radio, the great preference being for transistors.

Like radio, ownership of televisions is increasing, but still is low. Just under half the urban homes have a set, and less than one in ten in rural areas.

Television

Table 44 - Ownership of consumer durables
1975 and 1979 by urban/rural

	Total Philippines		Urban		Rural	
	1975	1979	1975	1979	1975	1979
	%	%	%	%	%	%
Households with a
Television	15	19	42	47	3	7
Black & White	15	19	41	44	3	7
Colour	1	2	3	5	*	*

Source: Consumer Pulse National Surveys

Penetration of television is as high among the ABCs as is radio, but below that tails off very sharply. Like radio the urban Es have fewer television sets than the rural people.

Television

Table 45 – Ownership of consumer durables
1975 and 1979 by socio-economic class
(Total urban Philippines)

	AB		C		D		E	
	1975	1979	1975	1979	1975	1979	1975	1979
	%	%	%	%	%	%	%	%
Household with a								
Television	98	98	90	90	35	46	3	4
Black & White	94	88	88	84	35	45	3	4
Colour	28	46	4	12	1	2	*	*

Source: Consumer Pulse National Surveys

Colour television is restricted almost entirely to the urban ABs, and penetration has doubled in the past five years.

Stereo ownership is almost as high as television penetration. Like television, there has been a rapid increase in rural ownership, although it is still very low.

Stereo

Table 46 – Ownership of consumer durables
1975 and 1979 by urban/rural

	Total Philippines		Urban		Rural	
	1975	1979	1975	1979	1975	1979
	%	%	%	%	%	%
Households with a						
Stereo	10	14	26	31	3	6

Source: Consumer Pulse National Surveys

Penetration of telephones is very low in the Philippines, and unlike other consumer durables it has decreased in the last five years. It is, and remains, almost zero outside the towns.

Telephone

Table 47 – Ownership of consumer durables
1975 and 1979 by urban/rural

	Total Philippines		Urban		Rural	
	1975	1979	1975	1979	1975	1979
	%	%	%	%	%	%
Households with a Telephone	5	4	15	12	*	*

Source: Consumer Pulse National Surveys

It might be supposed that this is due to the expansion of city population at the DE level through immigration from the countryside, but as the following table shows this is not in fact the case. The incidence of telephone ownership has largely declined at the AB and C levels.

Telephone

Table 48 – Ownership of consumer durables
1975 and 1979 by socio-economic class
(Total urban Philippines)

	AB		C		D		E	
	1975	1979	1975	1979	1975	1979	1975	1979
	%	%	%	%	%	%	%	%
Household with a Telephone	85	79	37	31	4	4	*	*

Source: Consumer Pulse National Surveys

Penetration of white goods is very low, even of refrigerators, which are almost entirely confined to the urban Philippines.

White goods

**Table 49 – Ownership of consumer durables
1975 and 1979 by urban/rural**

	Total Philippines		Urban		Rural	
	1975	1979	1975	1979	1975	1979
	%	%	%	%	%	%
Households with a						
Refrigerator	12	13	34	35	2	3
Freezer	1	2	3	3	*	1
Washing machine	1	*	2	1	-	-

Source: Consumer Pulse National Surveys

Refrigerator ownership falls off very sharply below the ABCs in urban areas.

White goods

**Table 50 – Ownership of consumer durables
1975 and 1979 by socio-economic class
(Total urban Philippines)**

	AB		C		D		E	
	1975	1979	1975	1979	1975	1979	1975	1979
	%	%	%	%	%	%	%	%
Household with a								
Refrigerator	96	98	84	88	21	27	1	1
Freezer	24	20	6	5	1	1	*	*
Washing machine	18	14	2	2	*	1	*	*

Source: Consumer Pulse National Surveys

The incidence of owning freezers and washing machines has declined in the ABs, and was already so low among the Cs that the drop there is negligible and not significant. This is an indication that despite the growing gap in the Philippines between the top and bottom of the income scale, increasing energy prices are having an effect at all levels.

Consistent with the low incline of washing machines, is the comparatively high proportion of homes with domestic help, which makes a washing machine superfluous.

Table 51 – Households with domestic help

	Total Philippines	Metro Manila	Other Urban	Rural
	%	%	%	%
Number of domestic servants				
1	6	16	9	3
2	2	6	2	*
3	1	1	1	*
4+	1	1	1	*/
None	90	76	87	97

Source: Consumer Pulse National Surveys

Use of stoves and water heaters is almost entirely confined to ABC homes in the urban areas.

Stoves and water heaters

Table 52 – Ownership of consumer durables
1975 and 1979 by urban/rural

	Total Philippines		Urban		Rural	
	1975	1979	1975	1979	1975	1979
	%	%	%	%	%	%
Households with a						
Stove	5	5	15	15	1	1
Water heater	NA	1	NA	2	NA	-

Source: Consumer Pulse National Surveys

Stoves and water heaters

Table 53 – Ownership of consumer durables
1975 and 1979 by socio-economic class
(Total urban Philippines)

	AB		C		D		E	
	1975	1979	1971	1979	1975	1979	1975	1979
	%	%	%	%	%	%	%	%
Household with a								
Stove	88	91	36	44	5	5	*	*
Water heater	NA	23	NA	3	NA	*	NA	-

Source: Consumer Pulse National Surveys

A similar situation applies to the ownership of air-conditioners, and the drop in the last five years because of increased energy costs is even more marked than for freezers and washing machines, because of the very high cost of running an air-conditioner.

Air conditioners

Table 54 – Ownership of consumer durables
1975 and 1979 by urban/rural

	Total Philippines		Urban		Rural	
	1975	1979	1975	1979	1975	1979
	%	%	%	%	%	%
Households with an						
Air conditioner	2	2	6	5	-	1

Source: Consumer Pulse National Surveys

Even among the urban ABs the incline has dropped substantially from two thirds to one half. In 1975, 67% of AB homes owned an air conditioner, but by 1979 this had dropped to 52%.

The use of motor cars in private ownership is very low in the Philippines. It is almost wholly confined to towns, and much the greater part is in Manila.

Motor cars

Table 55 – Ownership of consumer durables
1975 and 1979 by urban/rural

	Total Philippines		Urban		Rural	
	1975	1979	1975	1979	1975	1979
	%	%	%	%	%	%
Households with a motor car	4	3	11	10	*	*

Source: Consumer Pulse National Surveys

6 Tourist Markets

VISITOR ARRIVALS AND EXPENDITURE

Tourism is an important earner of foreign exchange for the Philippines, but as seventh highest earner does not occupy such a vital position as in some neighbouring countries where it is in second or third place. Foreign exchange receipts grew from US$238 million in 1979 to an estimated US$309 million in 1980, excluding earnings from returning Filipinos resident abroad.

Arrivals of foreign visitors topped 1 million in 1980, having shown steady growth throughout the last decade, but slowing down in 1980.

Table 56 - Foreign visitors arrivals to the Philippines

	Number	Growth per year
1970	144,071	16.9%
1975	418,860	23.7%
1976	478,822	14.3%
1977	626,662	30.9%
1978	725,850	15.8%
1979	966,873	33.2%
1980	1,003,764	3.8%

Source: Ministry of Tourism

In addition to these foreign visitors, there is a significant influx of Filipinos resident abroad, largely in the USA. In 1978 this totalled 133,546 and in the 12 months ending September 1980, 80,733.

The largest single overseas tourist supplier is Japan, followed by North America and Europe. Among the intermediate countries, Singapore and Malaysia are growing, both supplying more visitors than Germany, the largest European originator.

Table 57 – Country of origin of visitor arrivals, 1980
        (including returning Filipinos)

	Number		%
Japan	291,825		29.1
USA	147,421		14.7
Canada	15,474		1.5
Western Europe	149,858		14.9
Germany		28,157	
UK		22,749	
France		14,930	
Switzerland		13,412	
Italy		9,987	
Spain		8,063	
Other		52,560	
ASEAN	89,463		8.9
Hong Kong	76,973		7.7
Australia	46,831		7.7
Taiwan	37,511		3.7
Others	148,498		14.8
	1,003,764		100.0

Source: Ministry of Tourism

The average length of stay in the Philippines has grown slowly but steadily throughout the last two decades, as has average daily expenditure.   However, tourist daily expenditure increased by an index of 156 in 1978 against 100 in 1972, but over the same period the CPI rose to 215.   Therefore between 1972 and 1978 there was a decrease of approximately 28% in what the tourist dollar could buy, allowing for the CPI not being strictly comparable to tourist rates.

Nevertheless, by international standards Manila is extremely cheap for the tourist.   The UBS survey of 1980 gave Manila an index of 38 for restaurant costs and 44 for hotel costs compared with Zurich.

**Table 58 – Estimated tourist receipts
(including returning Filipinos)**

	Number of Visitors	Average Length of Stay (Days)	Average Individual Daily Expenditures US$
1960	50,657	6.4	30.00
1965	84,015	7.0	30.00
1970	144,071	7.3	30.50
1971	144,321	7.3	30.50
1972	166,431	7.3	31.50
1973	242,811	7.8	33.50
1974	410,138	7.8	33.50
1975	502,211	7.8	34.78
1976	615,159	8.1	43.06
1977	730,123	8.1	49.07
1978	859,396	8.1	49.07

Source: Ministry of Tourism

The typical foreign visitor is a man aged 20-59, and his purpose for visiting the Philippines is pleasure. Returning Filipinos are equally likely to be men or women, in the same mid-age group as the foreign nationals, but less likely to be returning solely for a pleasure trip.

Table 59 - Characteristics and purposes of visitor arrivals (1978)

	Foreign Visitors	Filipinos resident abroad
	725,850	133,546
	%	%
Men	72	46
Women	28	54
Age		
20 and less	8	8
20-39	47	54
40-59	35	26
60 and over	10	12
Purpose of visit		
Pleasure	79	57
Business	11	12
Official mission	2	5
Employment	*	8
Other	8	18

Source: Ministry of Tourism

The mode of arrival is almost entirely by air, and largely into Manila International Airport.

Table 60 - Visitor arrivals by mode of arrival (1978)

	859,396
	%
Air	98
Sea	2

Source: Ministry of Tourism

TOURIST PROMOTION

In 1973 the Ministry of Tourism was formed, with the objective of meeting targets for tourist arrivals and revenue receipts. By 1980 the arrivals total was below target, but receipts met target if returning Filipinos are included. The arrivals target for 1987 calls for a tripling of the 1980 actual figure.

Table 61 - Target versus actual tourist arrivals

(millions)	Target	Actual
1978	.86	.86
1979	1.01	.97
1980	1.19	1.00
1981	1.41	
1982	1.66	
1987	2.93	

Source: Ministry of Tourism

In 1980 the Ministry of Tourism promoted the Philippines in foreign markets, as a tourist destination at trade fairs, festivals and shows, and participated at international congresses. The promotion aims to sell the Philippines as a foremost congress centre.

The promotion campaign is divided into the following divisions.

Regional Dispersal

The regional dispersal programme is designed to upgrade transport and accommodation facilities, and to establish additional tourist attractions, in regions outside Manila, in order to try to direct tourist expenditure further afield outside the capital.

Domestic Promotions and Marketing Programmes

The promotion of travel by Filipinos and foreign visitors, within the Philippines. This is aimed at local households as well as returning Filipinos.

Tourism Assistance Programmes in Local Governments

A programme of technical assistance to organise local tourist boards in the provinces.

Convention Promotions

Intensive promotion gained three major international conferences for Manila in 1980 (PATA, ASTA, ASEAN Law Association) drawing an estimated 60,000 delegates. A total of 443 were held in the Philippines in 1980, 173 international and 270 national.

Manpower Development

A series of training courses and seminars for personnel at all levels in the tourist industry.

Aviation Developments

The new bilateral air agreement was reached between the Philippines and the USA, which has resulted in significant improvement in aviation services to and within the Philippines.

RESIDENTS' TRAVEL

282,892 passports for foreign travel were issued to Filipinos in 1980.

Half of these were for labourers and private employees under contractual work.

Labourers	78,046	28%
Private employees	63,153	22%

The three major destinations were the USA, Saudi Arabia and Hong Kong.

7 Finance Markets

The latest information published in NEDA shows a substantial increase in money supply in 1980 of 19.6% compared with the tightly controlled 11.2% of the previous year.

Table 62 – **Money supply and its origin**
          (Pesos millions)

	Money Supply	International Reserve	Domestic Credits	Non-money Supply Deposits	Miscellaneous Accounts (Net Balance)
1971	5,179.1	1,311.4	75,585.1	7,304.3	4,413.1
1972	6,469.5	1,890.3	17,693.1	8,103.0	5,010.9
1973	7,267.2	6,774.4	21,791.8	16,523.6	4,775.4
1974	9,007.8	8,248.5	30,919.8	22,874.4	7,826.1
1975	10,314.8	8,179.5	38,218.8	24,089.0	11,994.5
1976	12,074.9	8,691.8	46,003.7	29,034.7	13,585.9
1977	14,938.5	6,973.2	55,393.8	34,810.6	12,617.9
1978	16,945.4	6,768.1	68,550.3	42,906.9	15,466.0
1979	18,843.5	NA	NA	NA	NA
1980	22,537.5	(7,115.9)	95,128.3	48,392.1	17,082.8

Source: Central Bank of the Philippines

Inflation had reached an annual rate of 21.2% in February 1980, but according to the latest published data dropped to 14.6% in February 1981, based on the national consumer price index.

FINANCIAL SYSTEM

The financial system of the Philippines has been well regulated by government controls, and prior to 1980 had grown into one of the most complex and diverse systems in the region.   All sorts of different financial institutions exist with activities confined strictly in accordance with a specific, narrow charter permitted by one of many government acts. The result has been a proliferation of small specialised banking and financial institutions.

A major advance was achieved in 1980 in rationalising this complex structure, when the Universal Banking System was introduced. It is described at the end of this chapter.

Central Bank of the Philippines

Central to the banking and financial system is the Central Bank of the Philippines which has control over the banks and financial institutions with three main objectives; to maintain monetary stability, to hold the value and convertibility of the Peso, and to promote industry. The Central Bank provides the regulatory supervision of the banking system that the Securities and Exchange commission (SEC) provides over business enterprises.

Commercial Banks

By the end of 1980 there were 32 commercial banks in the Philippines; 27 of them private domestic banks, 4 private foreign banks and 1 government controlled. In addition to the 4 foreign banks, 24 foreign banks maintained regional or representative offices. By August 1979 the assets of the commercial banks exceeded Pesos 100 billion, over double the assets of the Central Bank, and they constitute the largest category of financial institutions in the country.

Offshore Banking Units

Offshore Banking Units (OBUS) were introduced in 1976, in an attempt to attract international and regional banking business to the Philippines, thereby setting Manila in competition against Hong Kong and Singapore. An OBU is a branch of a foreign bank licensed to transact banking business both off-shore and in the Philippines. By the end of 1980 there were 21 OBUs licensed to operate. OBUs are not subject to exchange control, and provide tax advantages.

Rural Banks

There are over 1,018 rural banks in the Philippines which provide loans to small farmers and merchants in related rural industries.

Private Development Banks

An unusual feature of the Philippines financial system is 44 private development banks which promote industrial and agricultural development with long-term loans, and also the provision of technical assistance.

Specialised Government Banks

There are three specialised banks operated by the government, primarily concerned with development and low financing projects.

Savings and Mortgage Banks, Stock Savings and Loan Associations

There are 10 Savings and Mortgage banks and 88 stock savings and loan associations.

In addition to these banks, there are large numbers of financial institutions operating quasi-banking services; financing companies, fund managers, investment companies and lending investors.

Stock Exchanges

In the Philippines there are three Stock Exchanges; the Manila Stock Exchange founded in 1927, the Makati Stock Exchange (1965) and the Metropolitan Stock Exchange (1974).

The Money Market

Established in 1961, the money market is a two-tier system for raising funds by selling IOUs or promissory notes to money market dealers for cash.

Universal Banking System

A major step in rationalising the complex financial institution of the Philippines was taken in 1980 with the enactment of the Universal Banking System. Seven existing banking laws were amended (Central Bank Charter, General Banking Act, Savings and Loan Association Act, Private Development Banks Act, Charter of the Development Bank of the Philippines, Rural Banks Act, Investment Houses Law).

The powers of the Central Bank of the Philippines were increased to enable it to supervise the reforms of the new system.

The essential purpose of the system is to eliminate the distinctions between all of the different types of banks, and to enable the new 'unibank' to offer the entire range of services, previously split into different categories and confined within it. It thus both simplifies the financial system of the Philippines, and by rationalising it opens the way for additional activity in the market.

Table 63 - Assets and Liabilities of financial institutions (August 1979, in Pesos millions)

	Total Assets	Total Liabilities
Central Bank	45,303.9	44,794.6
Commercial Banks	101,053.2	92,412.1
Savings Banks	4,816.2	4,816.2
Rural Banks[+]	4,554.8	3,801.1
Development Banks[+]	20,810.1	16,886.4

Source: Central Bank of the Philippines (+ June 1979)

8 Industrial Markets

INDUSTRY AND MANUFACTURING

One of the economic problems faced by the Philippines has been the failure of the manufacturing sector to increase its share of the country's GDP, and it has been stagnant despite active promotion by the authorities.

Table 64 – Manufacturing as a percentage of GDP

	1970	1975	1977	1978	1979
	%	%	%	%	%
Manufacturing as a % of GDP	22.6	24.9	24.3	24.1	24.3

Source: National Economic and Development Authority

In the total industrial sector of the economy, although manufacturing has not increased its share of GDP, construction and production of electricity and gas have. Despite this, there remains a chronic shortage of domestic housing, as seen in Chapter 3.

Within this overall picture however certain manufacturing industries have made substantial growth, notably; food and beverages (partly to use the country's sugar surplus), tobacco, textiles, paper, publishing and print, chemicals, petroleum products and transport equipment.

This is demonstrated in the following table, which shows an increase in the order of 50% in the amount of value added at constant prices for 1972. This increase has not however served to increase the GDP share contributed by manufacturing.

53

Table 65 - Gross value added in manufacturing by industry group (Pesos millions)

	1972	1975	1976	1977	1978
AT CURRENT PRICES:					
Food manufacturers	3,623	7,231	8,241	9,398	10,658
Beverage industries	724	1,264	1,429	1,689	1,959
Tobacco manufacturers	950	1,875	2,084	2,395	2,456
Textile manufacturers	798	1,687	2,154	2,364	2,690
Footwear, wearing apparel	431	834	982	1,130	1,489
Wood and cork products	582	871	1,148	1,632	1,694
Furniture and fixtures	86	131	156	180	202
Paper and paper products	345	826	1,009	1,130	1,207
Publishing and printing	265	557	608	617	652
Leather and leather products	22	42	50	59	62
Rubber products	220	400	398	425	442
Chemicals and chemical products	1,812	3,530	3,625	3,681	3,815
Products of petroleum and coal	1,048	3,526	3,625	3,681	3,815
Non-metallic mineral products	445	954	1,087	1,220	1,452
Basic metal industries	409	1,373	1,629	2,055	2,410
Metal products	401	678	729	946	1,079
Machinery except electrical	184	303	336	393	420
Electrical machinery	355	751	727	847	983
Transport equipment	516	1,447	1,586	1,801	2,176
Miscellaneous manufacturers	172	264	313	317	347
Gross value added in manufacturing	**13,388**	**28,544**	**32,545**	**37,834**	**42,607**
AT CONSTANT PRICES OF 1972:					
Food manufacturers	3,623	4,245	4,558	4,814	5,044
Beverage industries	724	808	859	1,020	1,100
Tobacco manufacturers	950	1,542	1,556	1,567	1,596
Textile manufacturers	798	923	1,097	1,104	1,258
Footwear, wearing apparel	431	591	628	657	768
Wood and cork products	582	471	558	714	715
Furniture and fixtures	86	74	79	83	84
Paper and paper products	345	486	538	547	547
Publishing and printing	265	447	455	424	435
Leather and leather products	22	39	31	33	34
Rubber products	220	263	232	227	227
Chemicals and chemical products	1,812	2,165	2,462	2,930	3,281
Products of petroleum and coal	1,048	1,230	1,134	1,069	1,108
Non-metallic mineral products	445	597	613	626	684
Basic metal industries	409	587	631	747	815
Metal products	401	398	389	465	492
Machinery except electrical	184	190	195	207	219
Electrical machinery	355	443	394	437	462
Transport equipment	516	842	854	923	997
Miscellaneous manufacturers	172	205	218	199	200
Gross value added in manufacturing	**13,388**	**16,537**	**17,481**	**18,793**	**20,066**

Source: National Census and Statistics Office

Capital investment has been particularly high in transport equipment, metal products, paper and print, textiles and food processing. This very much reflects government export promotions as well as investment incentives. The export diversification of electrical and metal products is a result of this.

Table 66 – Capital investments of newly registered business organizations engaged in manufacturing classified by kind of business

(Pesos '000s)

	1977		1978	
	Number	Paid in Capital	Number	Paid in Capital
Total	**4,705**	**356,383**	**6,352**	**539,302**
Food manufacturing	923	28,415	952	48,813
Sugar refineries	6	3,569	5	1,202
Coconut products	17	2,651	28	11,008
Beverages	29	616	5	172
Tobacco manufacturing	14	1,204	11	21,130
Textiles	177	17,340	726	37,843
Footwear (except rubber & wearing apparel)	548	21,427	149	20,169
Wood manufactures	317	21,116	484	21,257
Furniture and fixtures	233	5,936	360	12,433
Paper and paper products	18	2,345	68	6,722
Printing, publishing & allied industries	371	17,189	425	29,381
Leather & leather products (except footwear)	68	5,231	182	4,063
Rubber products	39	4,254	33	5,113
Drugs and chemical products	126	9,573	226	14,297
Non-metallic mineral products	240	11,365	274	26,671
Metal products	399	20,049	695	53,318
Machineries, apparatus, appliances & supplies	308	18,994	258	24,664
Transportation equipment	89	7,095	71	155,414
Others	783	158,014	400	54,631

Source: National Census and Statistics Office

The following table, of foreign exchange earnings shows a pattern consistent with this.

**Table 67 - Projected annual average net foreign exchange
earnings of BOI - Registered Firms**

	Average Annual Net Foreign Exchange Earnings ($'000s)	
	1978	1979
Total	**145,086**	**203,034**
Agro-based sector	**20,901**	**54,475**
Food and beverages	5,560	21,493
Crumb rubber	-	900
Wood products	5,923	19,394
Pulp and paper	-	12,688
Seeds	9,148	-
Mining & mineral processing sector	**9,880**	**NA**
Non-metallic products	9,880	NA
Metal based sector	**30,208**	**58,250**
Electric products	30,208	49,714
Metal products	-	5,097
Machinery, equipment & parts	-	1,203
Transport equipment & parts	-	1,058
Jewellry	-	1,178
Chemical-based sector	**78,485**	**75,410**
Plastic products	-	17,343
Footwear	39,806	22,913
Chemicals & chemical products	17,078	-
Textile products	6,845	1,671
Garments	14,756	32,483
Other products	**5,612**	**14,149**

Source: Board of Investment

The following table contains older data, and the picture will have changed since then in view of the investment in new business since 1977. However, it is broadly indicative of the number and distribution of manufacturing establishments in the Philippines, and the major contributors to output.

Table 68 – Number of establishments, employment and output value by industry group (1977)

	No . of Establishments	Employment (Average for the year)		Value of Gross Output (Pesos millions)
		Total	Paid Employees	
All Manufacturing Establishments	**74,621**	**778,131**	**675,831**	**67,826.1**
Food	26,546	179,467	139,757	17,622.8
Beverage	1,106	25,146	23,749	3,925.0
Tobacco	39	20,927	20,918	3,219.8
Textiles	3,157	97,993	92,709	5,154.2
Wearing apparel, except footwear	28,986	119,805	83,894	1,282.5
Leather and products of leather, leather substitutes and fur, except footwear and wearing apparel	219	2,939	2,568	93.6
Footwear, except rubber, plastic or wood footwear	1,294	9,605	7,534	123.9
Wood and cork products, except furniture	1,945	44,666	42,380	1,742.0
Furniture and fixtures, except primarily of metal	2,475	19,431	16,304	410.2
Paper and paper products	199	15,073	14,979	2,497.6
Printing, publishing and allied industries	1,131	17,611	16,340	1,003.3
Industrial chemicals	98	9,488	9,412	2,106.6
Other chemical products	282	23,457	23,364	4,348.0
Petroleum refineries	4	1,088	1,088	8,095.9
Miscellaneous products of petroleum and coal	11	318	308	178.4
Rubber products	265	11,601	11,280	969.4
Plastic products, n.e.c.	234	19,320	19,177	1,010.8
Pottery, china and earthenware	639	4,360	3,161	187.7
Glass and glass products	42	7,226	7,208	586.1
Other non-metallic mineral products	1,066	20,189	18,967	1,781.9
Iron and steel basic Industries	119	12,082	12,027	1,747.8
Non-ferrous metal basic industries	28	2,385	2,379	290.8
Fabricated metal products except machinery and equipment and furniture and fixtures primarily of metal	3,019	28,095	23,637	1,707.2
Machinery except electrical	821	16,732	15,938	643.0
Electrical machinery, apparatus, appliances and supplies	201	34,143	34,073	2,476.7
Transport equipment	635	25,644	25,009	3,385.6
Professional and scientific and measuring and controlling equipment not elsewhere classified, and of photographic and optical instruments	22	1,301	1,292	77.4
Other Industries	938	8,039	6,379	157.9

Source: National Census and Statistics Office

INDUSTRIAL DEVELOPMENT STRATEGY

The government have developed a strategy to encourage manufacturing and industrial development to the point of catching up with other sectors of the economy. This operates primarily through a series of organisations and government bodies with specific purposes, a list of priorities for industrial investment, and special incentives. These priorities and incentives are designed not only to encourage industrial development but also to channel it in line with secondary objectives such as export diversification, import substitution and creation of employment in areas without employment.

The more important of the government organisations, with authority to institute development procedures are as follows:

National Economic and Development Authority (NEDA)

This is a central planning office, empowered to draw up recommendations for economic and social planning, which are implemented by other bodies. It does have regulatory authority.

Export Processing Zone Authority (EPZA)

This body seeks to encourage foreign trade through the establishment of special zones suitable to export industries. They are located in various regions of the Philippines, and have suitable labour and transport facilities.

Board of Investments (BOI)

This is probably the major body seeking to promote investment in the Philippines. It was established with the following defined objectives.

"The Board of Investments is the government agency charged with the task of implementing four investment laws, namely: the Investment Incentives Act, the Export Incentives Act, the Foreign Business Regulations Act and the Agricultural Investment Incentives Act. These acts are designed to quicken the pace of industrialization and to raise the living standards of the people through increased economic opportunities and a more equitable distribution of the benefits of development.

Through a package of incentives, the establishment of projects that will effect dispersal of industries in the rural area, generate employment opportunities, promote labor-intensive manufactured goods for export, develop small and medium-scale industries and increase the utilization of indigenous raw materials are encouraged under the Investment Incentives Act. Projects with high linkage effects are given priority in order to close the gaps in the industrial structure. The law expressly welcomes and encourages foreign capital to establish pioneer enterprises which would utilize substantial amounts of domestic raw materials in joint venture with Filipino capital, whenever available.

The Export Incentives Act encourages the utilization of excess manufacturing capacities for export, particularly those that are labor-intensive. It also grants incentives to export trading houses which collect and export the products of fragmented and dispersed existing capacities. Similarly, service exporters like cargo transporters, legal consultancy firms and motion picture companies as well as facilities that cater primarily to foreign tourists are given support by the board. Exportable products that are entitled to incentives are listed in the annual Export Priorities Plan prepared by the Board.

The third law, the Foreign Business Regulations Act, covers the entry of foreign investments in areas of business activity not listed in the above Investment Priorities Plan or the Export Priorities Plan. Through this, the BOI is either to channel foreign investments away from areas which are already adequately exploited by Filipino nationals into areas which will contribute to the sound and balanced development of the economy.

The Agricultural Investments Incentives Decree was promulgated to further boost agro-industrial business and to accelerate the attainment of a reasonable degree of self-sufficiency in basic foodstuffs and essential raw materials. Thus, the decree provides additional incentives for agro-industrial projects beyond those already provided by the Investment Incentives Act. Following the measured capacity concept of the Investment and Export Incentives Acts, essential agricultural products, most of which are inputs into agro-industrial operations, are listed in the Agricultural Investment Priorities Plan."
(Board of Investments, September 1980)

The BOI seeks to meet these objectives through a series of five Priorities Plans which were enacted on May 13, 1980. The following are extracts from the relevant BOI handbooks (which can be obtained with complete details from the Asia Pacific Centre in London)

The Thirteenth Investment Priorities Plan

"The Thirteenth Investment Priorities Plan lists preferred areas of activity in the manufacturing sector where investments are being encouraged. Investments in projects listed in the Plan are entitled to the set of incentives granted under the Investment Incentives Act. Although these projects are generally oriented toward the domestic market, exportation of products with export potential is encouraged once the domestic demand has been met. The total amount of registrable capacity for each area is indicated by the measured capacity.

The general policy objectives enunciated in the investment laws and the Four-Year Development Plan continue to be the primary consideration in the selection of priority projects. These objectives are: promotion of labor-intensive projects, regional dispersal of industries, development of small and medium-scale industries and promotion of manufactured exports.

For the Thirteenth IPP, the Board has adopted the policy of promoting major industrial programs instead of industry sectors. Restructuring the IPP around major priority programs would facilitate the formulation of more comprehensive plans for each industrial program. These would include an enunciation of the objectives specific to each program and the timing of inclusion of projects supporting the program.

Some essential projects, though not supportive of these programs, have been retained because they support other national priority programs, such as the development of self-reliance in food and other essential products."

The priorities listed are:

Word processing
Mineral processing
Steel mill

Copper mill

Motorcycle manufacturing

Car and truck manufacturing

Shipbuilding

Engineering industries

Nitrogeneous and phosphate fertilizers

Linkages to the above

Agro-industries

Chemical industries

The Sixth Public Utilities Priorities Plan

"Presidential Decree No. 485, which amended the Investment Incentives Act and the Export Incentives Act, provided for the inclusion of public utilities among the list of projects that are eligible to receive incentives under the Investment Incentives Act. Public utilities fulfill a basic role in our economic development program. The development of the industry would ultimately benefit the final consumers since incentives granted to the industry would offset the high costs which deter expansion and replacement of obsolete and inefficient facilities of the industry."

Public utilities listed are:

Inter-island shipping

Electric utilities

1980 Energy Priorities Program

"The Energy Priorities Program lists preferred areas of activities where the potential for utilization of coal and non-conventional sources of energy can be best promoted. These projects are entitled to the incentives granted under the Investment Incentives Act, the Export Incentives Act, the Agricultural Investment Incentives Act, whichever incentive law would be appropriate, as well as the benefits under P.D. 1584 accruing to all BOI-registered enterprises and P.D. 1968 whenever applicable.

Projects registered under the Export Priorities Plan shall be exempt from the provisions of P.D. 1395. They shall be accorded priority by all government-owned or controlled financing institutions such as, but not limited to, the Central Bank of the Philippines, Development Bank of the Philippines, Philippine National Bank and applications for financial assistance submitted for these projects shall be given preferential consideration in the matter of collateral requirements, rediscounting and other requirements in order to facilitate the early establishment of the projects. Furthermore, cost incurred in the establishment and construction of non conventional energy conversion facilities or equipment duly certified by the Ministry of Energy may, at the option of the taxpayer, be directly chargeable to expenses and shall be fully deductible as such from gross income in the year wherein such expenses were incurred."

The energy priorities are as follows:

Alcohol production

Conversion of biomass materials

Establishment and conversion of manufacturing plant using coal, geothermal energy

Manufacture of equipment necessary in energy production from coal, geothermal sources, alcohol, biomass

Manufacture of solar energy devices

Manufacture of small-scale hydroelectric turbines

Manufacture of windmills

Any plant using non-conventional energy

The Third Agricultural Investment Priorities Plan

"In line with the new emphasis on rural agricultural development, the Agricultural Investment Incentives Decree was promulgated in June 1977, the express objective of which is to strengthen and stabilize the economic, political and social structure of the country by diffusing productive employment and income opportunities to the countryside and increasing the production and export of food products and raw-material inputs for industries.

As in the other two Investment Acts (R.A.'s 5186 and 6135), the Agricultural Investment Incentives Decree provides the mechanics for drawing up an annual Agricultural Investment Priorities Plan jointly by the Board of Investments and the Ministry of Agriculture.

The Agricultural Investment Incentives Decree is open to any individual, corporation, partnership, cooperative or other entity organized and existing under Philippine law, as long as it is engaged in the pursuit of agricultural activities and/or services, including food processing where the final product involves or will involve the substantial use and processing of domestic agro-based raw materials."

The plan seeks to encourage the following:

Food production
Production and/or processing of feed and feed ingredients
Production of certified and hybrid seeds and breeders
Farm services

The Eleventh Export Priorities Plan

"The Eleventh Export Priorities Plan is a listing of products currently being developed and promoted because of their existing and/or potential markets. The products included are those which would increase foreign exchange earnings, encourage utilization of excess manufacturing capacities for export, develop new markets, utilize indigenous raw materials, create employment opportunities and effect regional dispersal of industries.

The Plan is divided into List A which contains a range of exportable products of existing firms and List B, which lists products whose export potential warrants government support and promotion.

Export producers and traders of these products qualify for incentives under the Export Incentives Act. Incentives are also given to service exporters for preferred export service areas."

List A: Exportable products of existing firms.

Food products
Wood products
Paper products
Fibre products

Processed rubber

Chemicals and chemical products

Pharmaceutical products

Textiles

Non-metallic products

Metallic products

Machinery, equipment and parts

Electrical products, machines and parts

List B: Exportable products of preferred areas of investment

Food products

Vegetable oils

Animal feeds

Processed rubber

Leather products

Metallic mineral products

Non-metallic mineral products

Chemicals and chemical products

Textiles

Fabricated metal products

Non-electrical machinery

Electrical products, machines and parts

Transport equipment

Within each of these categories, both for List A and List B there is a list of individual items, totalling several hundreds in all.

Export Incentives Act and Investment Incentives Act

Within the exception of the Agricultural Priorities Plan, incentives available are as listed for the two Incentives Acts, which are as follows:

I. Registered Enterprises

	Export Incentives Act			Investment Incentives Act		
	Export Producer	Export Trader	Service Exporter	Filipino-owned		Foreign-owned
				Pioneer	Non-Pioneer	Pioneer

A. Rights & Guarantees to Registered Enterprises

1. Basic rights and guarantees under the Constitution;	x	x	x	x	x	x
2. Right to repatriate investments and remit earnings*;	x	x	x	x	x	x
3. Right to remit foreign exchange to service foreign loans and obligations arising from technological assistance contracts*;	x	x	x	x	x	x
4. Freedom from expropriation of property except for public use, national welfare and defense and upon payment of just compensation; and	x	x	x	x	x	x
5. Freedom from requisition of investment, except in event of war or national emergency and only for the duration thereof and with just compensation.	x	x	x	x	x	x

B. Incentives to Registered Enterprises

1. Deduction of organizational and pre-operational expenses from taxable income over a period of not more than 10 years from start of operation;	x			x	x	x
2. Deduction of labor training expenses from taxable income equivalent to 1/2 of expenses but not more than 10% of direct labor wage;	x[5]	.		x	x	x
3. Accelerated depreciation;	x			x	x	x
4. Carry-over as deduction from taxable income of net operating losses incurred in any of the first 10 years of operation deductible for the six years immediately following the year of such loss;	x[3]	x[3]		x	x	x
5. Exemption/reduction and/or deferment of tariff duties and compensating tax on importations of machinery, equipment and spare parts;	x[5][16]	x[6][16]		x[11][16]	x[10][16]	x[11][16]
6. Tax credit equivalent to 100% of the value of compensating tax & customs duties that would have been paid on machinery, equipment and spare parts (purchased from a domestic manufacturer), had these items been imported;	x[5]		x[6]	x	x	x

65

Incentive	1	2	3	4	5	6
7. Tax credit for tax withheld on interest payments on foreign loans provided such credit is not enjoyed by lender-remitee in his country and registered enterprise has assumed liability for tax-payment;				x	x	x
8. Right to employ foreign nationals in supervisory, technical or advisory positions within five years from registration;	x[14]			x	x	x
9. Deduction from taxable income in the year reinvestment was made of a certain percentage of the amount of undistributed profits or surplus transferred to capital stock for procurement of machinery and equipment and other expansion;	x[5]			x	x	x
10. Anti-dumping protection;	x[5]			x	x	x
11. Protection from government competition;	x[5]			x	x	x
12. Exemption from all taxes under the National Internal Revenue Code, except income tax on a gradually diminishing percentage;	x[2] 16			x[16]		x[16]
13. Post-operative tariff protection;	x[2]			x		x
14. Tax credits equivalent to sales, compensating and specific taxes and duties on supplies, raw materials and semi-manufactured products used in the manufacture, processing or production of export products;	x	x	x[1]	x	x	x
15. Additional deduction from taxable income of direct labor cost and local raw materials utilized in the manufacture of export products but not exceeding 25% of total export sales for traders; and 50% of total export fees for service exporters;	x[7]	x	x	x[9]	x[9]	x[9]
16. Additional deduction from taxable income an amount equivalent to expenses in establishing and maintaining an overseas office for the first five years of operation;		x[17]				
17. Exemption from sales taxes on export products sold to other export producers of export traders;	x[15]					
18. Preference in the grant of government loans;	x[5][12][14]	x[12][14]	x[12][14]		x	
19. Employment of foreign nationals within five years from operation or even after said period in exceptional cases;	x[2][14]					
20. Exemption from export and stabilization taxes;	x[16]	x[16]				
21. Additional deduction from taxable income of 1% of incremental export sales; and	x[3][4]	x[3][4]				
22. Additional incentives wherever processing or manufacturing plant is located in an area designated by BOI as necessary for proper dispersal of industry or which is deficient in infrastructures, public utilities and other facilities.	x[8]					

II.   INVESTORS IN REGISTERED ENTERPRISES

	Export Incentives Act						Investment Incentives Act			
	Filipino			Foreign			Filipino		Foreign	
Incentives to Investors	Export Prod.	Export Trader	Service Exp.	Export Prod.	Export Trader	Service Exp.	Pioneer	Non-Pioneer	Pioneer	Non-Pioneer
1. Basic rights and guarantees;	x	x	x	x	x	x	x	x	x	x
2. Right to repatriate investments and remit earnings*;	x	x	x	x	x	x	x	x	x	x
3. Freedom from expropriation of property;	x	x	x	x	x	x	x	x	x	x
4. Freedom from requisition of investments;	x	x	x	x	x	x	x	x	x	x
5. Protection of patents and other proprietary rights;	x	x	x	x	x	x	x	x	x	x
6. Exemption from capital gains tax on disposition of capital assets provided proceeds of sales are invested in new issues of capital stock of a registered enterprise within six months from the date gains were realized;	x[13]	x[14]	x[14]	x	x[14]	x[14]	x	x	x[13]	x
7. Tax allowance to the extent of actual investment but not to exceed 10% of taxable income;	x[2]						x			
8. Tax exemption on sale of stock dividends provided sale occurs within 7 years from date of registration;	x[2]						x			
9. Preference in the grant of GSIS and SSS loans for purchase of shares (for members only)	x[5]						x	x		

III. SPECIAL INCENTIVES FOR LESS DEVELOPED AREA REGISTERED ENTERPRISES

1.   Additional incentives to less developed area registered enterprises in the form of all incentives provided for a pioneer registered enterprise under its laws of registration, provided that less developed area registered enterprises engaged in non-pioneer activities shall not be exempt from the payment of sales taxes.

2.   Tax allowance to the extent of actual investment but not to exceed thirty percent (30%) of taxable income, inclusive of the normal tax allowance under its law of registration.*[1]

3.   Financial assistance in the form of preferences in the grant of liberalized loans to less developed area registered enterprise.*[2]

4. Exemption from the provisions of the General Banking Act with respect to collateral requirements.*[3]

5. Exemption from the payment of filing, processing and all other fees of the Board of Investments and of the Securities and Exchange Commission of all less developed area registered enterprises with total assets worth less than one million (P1,000,000) pesos.

---

*1. Except in mining ventures and provided that the investment is made in subscribed shares in the original and/or increased capital stock of an enterprise within seven years from the date of registration on a less developed area registered enterprise, and that the shares are held for a period of not less than three (3) years.

*2. Applicable to enterprises of either sole proprietorship of Filipino citizens or 60 percent Filipino-owned, or 60 percent Filipino-owned corporation or cooperatives.

*3. Section 78, Gen. Banking Act provides that loans against real estate security shall not exceed 70% of the appraised value of the respective real estate security plus 70% of the appraised value of insured improvements and such loans shall not be made unless title to the real estate, free from all encumbrances shall be with the mortgagor.

---

*Subject to Central Bank Regulations.

(1) Applicable to service exporters producing and exporting television and motion pictures or musical recording and catering primarily to foreign tourists (Tourism Incentives are now granted by the Philippine Tourism Authority).

(2) Provided registered export producer is engaged in a pioneer area.

(3) Applicable whenever a registered export producer and export trader shall

use a brand name for an export product that distinguishes it from products produced outside the Philippines.

(4) Applicable whenever financial assistance is extended by an export trader to export producers in an amount equivalent to not less than 20% of the export trader's export sales during the year.

(5) In general, applicable only to all projects for expansion or upgrading of export products under List A of the Export Priorities Plan and to both pioneer and non-pioneer under List B.

(6) Same as No. (1) but limited to expansion projects only and to service exporters catering primarily to foreign tourists. (Tourism Incentives are now granted by the Philippine Tourism Authority).

(7) Applicable to all registered export producers, except foreign firms in non-pioneer areas exporting 70% of their production.

(8) Additional incentives consist of using an amount equivalent to double the export producer's direct labor cost in applying the reduced income tax formula and/or tax credit on infrastructure.

(9) In the case of traditional exports, local raw material component is not included in the computation of said deduction.

(10) Applicable to new and expanding non-pioneer projects with total assets not exceeding P500,000 for the first two years of commercial operation. Non-pioneer projects with assets exceeding said amount and expanding non-pioneer projects with less than 20% return on equity are entitled only to reduced tariff and compensating tax, on a deferred payment basis for a period not exceeding 10 years. Expanding non-pioneer projects with 20% or greater return on equity shall be entitled to mere deferment of taxes and duties without any reduction thereof.

(11) Applicable to new or expanding pioneer projects with less than 20% return on equity. Expanding pioneer projects with 20% or greater return on equity and existing pioneer projects desiring to replace and modernize their

facilities are entitled to mere deferment of taxes and duties without any reduction thereof.

(12) Applicable to enterprises at least 60% Filipino-owned.

(13) More liberal terms, e.g. shorter holding period required of Filipino investors in pioneer projects.

(14) Grant of incentives would depend on the extent of operations registered with the BOI.

(15) Subject to guidelines formulated by the Board of Investments in consultation with the Bureau of Internal Revenue.

(16) Provided that the Board of Investments may increase the rate of tax exemption to not more than 50% of the tax exemption enjoyed by the registered enterprises prior to the increase, subject to any or all of the criteria provided for in Executive Order No. 569.

(17) Provided the Central Bank shall provide the necessary foreign exchange required to maintain such overseas offices of a registered export trader.

Assistance Team for Foreign Investments

This special unit was created within BOI in 1972, and is intended to assist foreign investors at three stages:

At the time the pre-investment survey is made

After the investment decision has been made and prior to setting up the plant

When the project is already operational and facilitation services are required

ATFI offers information and will also facilitate procedures. The services offered are as follows:

'Information' :-
The Team is in a position to provide information on such basic questions as:

Investment opportunities for foreign investors

Forms of desired foreign investments

Basic rights and guarantees given by Government to protect foreign investments

Incentives to foreign investors and methods of availment

Preferred sites for factories and plants

Suitable local partners

Registration requirements and procedures

Remittance of earnings

Repatriation of investments

Employment of foreign nationals

Government assistance in manpower training

Pertinent Philippine laws

'Facilitative' :-

Securities and Exchange Commission

Registration of partnership or incorporation papers

Board of Investments

Securing authority to do business

Registration for incentives availment

Central Bank of the Philippines

Registration of foreign investments

Remittance of earnings

Repatriation of investments

Import/Export procedures

Local Governments

Securing necessary municipal permits, clearances & licenses

Bureau of Customs

Claims for customs duty drawback

Application for bonded manufacturing warehouse
Importation of machinery and equipment
Importation of raw materials

Bureau of Internal Revenue

Tax structure
Tax incentives
Tax treaties

Ministry of Labour

Labour legislations
Labour-management relations

Commission on Immigration

Processing of applications for the entry of aliens as investors, management staff or technicians.

National Housing Authority

Visits to industrial estates
Selection of suitable sites in government-owned industrial estates

Ministry of Human Settlements

Securing locational clearance for new factories

Export Processing Zone Authority

Visits to the Zone
Registration as a Zone enterprise

9 Agricultural Markets

Agriculture is an important part of the economy of the Philippines for several reasons. Firstly, technological developments have in the last few years brought the country to the state of self sufficiency in food. Secondly, agricultural exports have traditionally, and continue to be a crucial earner of foreign exchange. Thirdly, because agricultural exports are not yet adequately diversified in terms of product or purchasing country, the balance of trade is extremely vulnerable to the constant shifts in world market prices.

Agricultural production in the Philippines is classified into food crops, and commercial crops, the latter being the major export earner.

RICE

The largest single crop produced is palay the rough rice crop of the Philippines, and the country has been self sufficient since 1977, and even created a surplus for export. Over half the agricultural land in the country is under rice cultivation.

This has been achieved with plant technology, which has been widely publicised, and through planting and irrigation schemes, and agrarian reform schemes. The plant technology for which the Philippines is famous is 'miracle rice'. Still the yields in the Philippines are among the lowest in Asia, and much needs to be done.

There has been considerable activity, less dramatic than 'miracle rice', in the area of land redistribution, farmer schemes, marketing improvements and development of small-farmer technology. Agricultural unemployment and seasonal hours remain serious parts of the problem of low productivity.

Table 69 - Quantity and value of crop production

	1975 Qty	1975 Value	1978 Qty	1978 Value
Total	**19,807.3**	**20,147.5**	**26,095.9**	**26,831.0**
Food crops	**13,549.0**	**13,421.2**	**18,371.0**	**18,131.6**
Palay (rough type)	5,660.1	5,345.5	6,894.9	6,794.1
Corn	2,568.4	2,153.2	2,855.2	2,729.4
Banana	1,686.0	1,542.6	3,155.8	1,510.4
Mango	239.3	254.8	335.2	678.4
Pineapple	424.4	504.1	464.9	707.0
Other fruit & nuts	337.4	569.2	506.4	825.5
Citrus	77.9	102.5	122.7	263.8
Rootcrops	1,807.1	811.8	3,004.4	1,060.2
Vegetables	444.6	1,000.9	489.2	745.0
Beans &peas	34.9	129.6	41.1	162.7
Coffee	91.4	647.1	118.8	1,871.8
Cacao	3.3	35.3	3.1	78.8
Peanuts	36.2	98.5	37.8	116.1
Others	138.0	226.1	341.5	588.4
Commercial crops	**6,258.3**	**6,726.3**	**7,724.9**	**8,699.4**
Coconut	1,723.1	2,895.5	4,194.8	4,398.5
Sugar	3,287.6	2,988.5	3,282.1	3,661.8
Abaca	133.6	514.1	129.8	240.1
Tobacco	57.1	242.2	56.7	270.8
Ramie	1.4	2.8	1.4	3.2
Rubber	45.7	74.0	54.4	109.8
Magusy	1.8	1.2	3.3	2.8
Others	8.0	8.0	2.4	12.4

Source: National Economic and Development Authority

CORN

The second major agricultural food product achieved production of 3.12 million metric tons in 1980. Although there was still a need to import a small quantity to meet livestock feeding rquirements, self-sufficiency has been achieved for human consumption.

COCONUT

Coconut is the major single foreign exchange earner and the Philippines has been able to export a substantial proportion of its production. The stock of coconut trees has been aging and production rates have been declining. The government is keenly aware of the importance of this crop and has launched a replanting programme, where 8,000 hectares, currently stocked with old and diseased trees, will be replanted with high-yielding and early-maturing hybrids.

The Philippines accounted for approximately a third of world production of coconuts in 1979. The government's target is to double production by 1990.

SUGAR

The world market price of sugar has fluctuated severely, with serious consequences for the Philippines balance of payments. However the price recovered in 1980, with the result that export earnings for sugar were almost $2\frac{1}{2}$ times the previous year's, while volume only increased about one third. There is a programme to increase the refining capacity in the Philippines substantially.

TIMBER

Forestry products are important earners of foreign exchange, although in 1980 they lagged behind the commercial crops, coconuts and sugar. There has been concern at the rate of deforestation, and in common with many other timber rich countries, over-cutting of this important resource. Export of logs and cutting of timber have been strictly controlled by the government. However, the government has been active in forest administration, conservation, research and development. Deforestation has been slowed down and 80,100 hectares have been reforested.

Table 70 - Quantity of production of logs, lumber, plywood and veneer (1,000 cu.m.)

		Logs	Lumber	Plywood	Veneer
	1970-71	10,679.5	860.4	652.7	242.0
	1975-76	8,440.7	n.a.	422.5	271.9
CY	1976	8,645.8	1,609.2	416.4	403.4
	1977	7,873.5	1,567.4	489.3	496.4
	1978	7,168.5	1,780.6	490.2	546.3

Source: Bureau of Forest Development

FISHERIES

An Intergrated Fisheries Development Plan was launched in 1976, with a target of accelerating fish production by 5.5% annually, and this was attained in 1980. The Plan involves training of municipal fishermen, the establishment of sea-farms, restocking of depleted waters particularly those caused by typhoon damage, and the establishment of fish farms and ponds. Production has been raised 50% in the last decade and export earnings over twelve times.

Table 71 – Quantity and value of fish production by type of production
(Quantity in thousand metric tons; value in Pesos millions)

	Total		Commercial Fishing Vessels		Fishponds		Municipal Fishing and Sustenance Fishing	
	Quantity	Value	Quantity	Value	Quantity	Value	Quantity	Value
1970	988.9	1,725.2	381.9	614.8	96.5	252.7	510.5	857.7
1975	1,336.8	5,919.1	498.6	2,549.0	106.5	809.1	731.7	2,561.0
1976	1,393.5	7,298.0	508.2	2,697.8	112.8	845.7	772.5	3,754.5
1977	1,508.9	8,809.2	518.2	3,543.2	115.8	891.3	874.9	4,374.7
1978	1,580.4	9,477.2	505.8	3,465.2	118.7	949.4	955.9	5,062.6

Source: National Economic and Development Authority

10 External Trade

BALANCE OF TRADE

The Philippines has suffered from a negative balance of foreign trade almost every year since the Second World War, before which there was always a favourable trade balance.   In common with other countries with low energy supplies, 1974 was a landmark when the cost of imports doubled over the 1973 level, due to world-wide inflation and the rise in oil prices, wiping out the small positive balance of 1973.

Table 72 - Exports and Import balance
(US$ millions)

	Net	Exports	Imports
1970	(28.4)	1,061.7	1,090.1
1971	(49.6)	1,136.4	1,186.0
1972	(124.1)	1,105.5	1,229.6
1973	289.7	1,886.3	1,596.6
1974	(418.3)	2,725.0	3,143.3
1975	(1,164.7)	2,294.5	3,459.2
1976	(1,059.8)	2,573.7	3,633.5
1977	(763.9)	3,150.9	3,914.8
1978	(1,307.3)	3,424.9	4,732.2
1979	(1,541.0)	4,601.0	6,142.0
1980	(1,901.1)	5,724.6	7,625.7

Source: National Census and Statistics Office

Imbalance has been aggravated by a fast growth rate in energy consumption relative to national output.   The result has been a steadily increasing trade deficit.   Although domestic industry has been growing, this in itself fuels the demand for energy, and makes exporting more expensive.

DIRECTION OF TRADE

The major trading partners of the Philippines have traditionally been the US and Japan. But in 1980 the Middle East moved into the second position as suppliers, just overtaking Japan, although total trade with the region remained only in fourth position because of low exports from the Philippines.

Table 73 – Direction and value of trade
(f.o.b. value in US$ millions)

	1979		1980	
	Exports	Imports	Exports	Imports
	4,601	6,142	5,635	7,814
United States	1,384	1,402	1,510	1,796
Japan	1,201	1,398	1,527	1,566
European Economic				
Community	931	851	960	905
West Germany	226	276	243	355
Netherlands	360	98	356	131
United Kingdom	136	195	141	193
Others	209	282	220	226
Middle East countries	61	964	131	1,570
Iraq	20	182	66	269
Kuwait	2	282	5	357
Saudi Arabia	20	368	25	765
Others	19	132	35	179
ASEAN countries	188	363	326	491
Indonesia	46	182	58	180
Malaysia	57	90	92	145
Singapore	66	81	113	147
Thailand	19	10	63	19
Socialist countries	144	152	267	215
People's Republic of China	51	121	45	190
U.S.S.R.	83	8	211	13
Others	10	23	11	12
Other countries	692	1,012	914	1,271
Hong Kong	158	153	190	190
South Korea	141	90	217	142
Australia	94	206	93	217
Taiwan	69	173	96	193
Others	230	390	318	529

Source: National Census and Statistics Office

COMPOSITION OF IMPORTS AND EXPORTS

Philippine exports have until recent years been made up with a small number of agricultural and primary commodities; coconut products, of which it is the world leader, timber, sugar, minerals, and a large number of small products. A major problem has been the volatility of world commodity prices. In 1980 the export in metric tons of sugar products increased to 131.6% of the 1979 volume, but the value to 273% of 1979's dollar earnings. This vulnerability has been made worse by the Philippine's dependence on a comparatively small number of traditional export commodities. However in the last decade there have been rapid increases in the contribution made by manufactured goods and non-traditional non-manufactures to the export performance of the Philippines

Table 74 – Manufactured goods, re-exports and non-traditional non-manufactured as a percentage of total exports

	1970	1975	1978	1979	1980
% of total exports	4.2%	19.0%	32.4%	40.8%	43.3%

Source: National Economic and Development Authority

The significant increases in manufactured exports have been in electrical and electronic components, garments, handicrafts, food products and beverages, furniture, footwear and chemicals. The target is that these should account for 50% of exports by 1987.

This is very largely the result of an aggressive policy instituted by the government to diversify the Philippine's export pattern in order to reduce over-dependence on certain sectors.

Table 75 – Exports by commodity
(f.o.b. value in US$ millions)

	1970	1975	1976	1977	1978	1979	1980
Total	1062	2294	2574	3151	3425	4601	5635
Coconut Products	209	466	540	761	908	965	768
Copra	80	172	150	201	136	89	57
Coconut oil	96	231	299	412	621	683	525
Desiccated coconut	19	30	37	90	82	107	117
Copra meal or cake	14	33	54	58	69	86	79
Sugar and Sugar Products	196	616	456	535	216	239	652
Centrifugal and refined sugar	188	581	429	512	197	212	620
Molasses	8	34	24	20	16	27	32
Others	*	1	3	3	3	*	*
Forest Products	295	260	308	294	362	484	406
Logs	237	167	135	134	145	144	90
Lumber	13	27	68	67	85	198	175
Plywood	20	21	43	41	72	107	101
Others	25	45	62	52	60	35	40
Mineral Products	224	256	306	430	478	566	802
Copper concentrates	185	212	266	268	250	440	545
Iron ore	3	1	-	-	-	-	-
Iron concentrates	10	12	7	-	-	-	-
Chromite ore	9	13	15	25	25	23	32
Others	17	19	18	137	203	103	225
Fruits and Vegetable	34	124	142	157	177	216	239
Pineapple products	22	41	52	64	74	74	86
Bananas	5	73	76	72	86	98	108
Others	7	10	14	21	17	44	45
Abaca and Products	17	22	27	29	25	42	44
Abaca unmanufactured	15	15	18	18	15	25	28
Abaca rope	2	7	9	11	10	17	16
Tobacco and Products	15	35	29	29	30	33	31
Raw tobacco	14	34	28	28	29	32	30
Cigars and others	1	1	1	1	1	1	1
Mineral Fuels and Lubricants	17	37	34	37	30	36	80
Chemicals	5	21	26	51	59	112	115
Textiles	5	22	28	21	31	29	58
Miscellaneous Manufactures and Others & Re-exports	45	435	678	807	1109	1879	2440

Sources: National Census and Statistics Offices, Central Bank of the Philippines

Table 76 – Non-traditional manufactured exports
(f.o.b. value in US$ millions)

	1979	1980
Electrical and electronic equipment and components	412	640
– Telecommunications and sound recording and reproduction apparatus and equipment	16	20
– Electrical machinery and parts	91	104
– Semiconductors and other micro-components	305	516
Garments	404	475
Handicrafts	134	150
Food products and beverages	57	83
Machinery and transport equipment	47	45
– Machinery specialized for particular industries	7	7
– Chassis, frames and other parts for motor vehicles	33	24
– Others	7	14
Furniture and parts	55	75
Footwear	59	64
Builders' woodwork and other wood manufacturers, excluding plywood, veneer and lumber	31	42
Nonmetallic mineral manufactures, particularly cement	. 31	53
Others: of which	171	267
Watches and clocks	12	29
Optical goods	1	2
Toys, games, sporting goods, and others	7	30
Household fixtures	3	2
Total	1401	1894

Sources: National Census and Statistics Office

Table 77 - Non-traditional non-manufactured exports
(f.o.b. value in US$ millions)

	1979	1980
Nickel	92	135
Iron ore agglomerates	120	115
Rice	47	65
Fish simply preserved	87	119
Others	132	112
Total nontraditional nonmanufactures	478	546

Source: National Census and Statistics Office

Table 78 - Imports by commodity group
(f.o.b. value in US$ millions)

	1979	1980
Capital Goods	1,785	1,977
Nonelectrical machinery	935	977
Electrical machinery	229	311
Transport equipment	329	274
Aircraft, ships & boats	215	301
Professional, scientific and controlling instruments	77	114
Raw Materials & Intermediate Goods	2,476	2,853
Wheat	106	138
Crude materials, inedible	260	274
Cotton	36	48
Synthetic & artificial fibers	75	60
Others	149	166
Animal & vegetable oils and fats	19	21
Chemicals	670	763
Chemical compound	249	275
Medicinal & pharm.chem.	61	70
Urea	51	73
Fertilizer excl. urea	40	63
Others	269	282
Manufactures	945	1,000
Paper & paper products	62	69
Textile yarn, fabrics and made-up articles	117	141
Iron and steel	438	422
Metal products	128	112
Others	200	256
Embroideries	125	138
Materials & accessories for the manufacture of elect. eqpt.	351	519
Mineral Fuels & Lubricants	1,385	2,359
Coal, coke and briquettes	14	24
Petroleum crude	1,115	1,988
Others	256	347
Consumer Goods	**496**	**625**
Food and live animals chiefly for food	248	327
Dairy products	96	113
Fish & fish preparations	20	22
Rice	-	-
Corn	4	35
Others	128	157
Beverages & tobacco	48	51
Miscellaneous excl. professional scientific & controlling instruments	64	70

Live animals, n.e.s.	136	177
Articles temporarily imported or exported	78	104
Others	58	78
Total	**6,142**	**7,814**

Source: National Census and Statistics Office

FOREIGN TRADE POLICY

The Five Year Philippine Development Plan 1978-1982 laid out five objectives for the foreign trade sector.

1) increase export earnings;

2) import commodities in an amount sufficient to support the essential consumer and production requirements;

3) include more processed and labor-intensive products in the composition of exports;

4) diversify export markets and import sources;

5) disperse export development to the regions.

In order to reach these objectives a series of fiscal (taxation), financial and institutional policies is being pursued.

11 Labour Force

COMPOSITION OF THE LABOUR FORCE

The Philippines has a labour force of approximately 17 million men and women. Although there is plenty of statistical information about the labour force, it usually has a two to three year lag before publication. However, changes in the labour force are not as rapid as some other economic parameters that the businessman needs to monitor, and the data is probably sufficient for the purposes of this book. The latest information available was published in April 1981 at time of going to press, and refers to the period of the second quarter of 1978.

Table 79 - Labour force by work status
(15 years and over)

	1977 1st quarter	1977 3rd quarter	1977 4th quarter	1978 1st quarter	1978 2nd quarter
('000s)					
a. In the Labor Force	15,989	15,002	14,994	15,386	16,757
1. Employed	14,985	14,334	14,323	14,588	15,699
(a) In Agriculture	7,046	7,474	7,308	7,315	8,054
(b) In Non-Agricultural Industries	7,939	6,860	7,015	7,274	7,645
2. Totally Unemployed	1,004	668	671	798	1,058
(a) Worked Before	587	343	396	424	612
(b) Never Worked Before	417	325	275	374	446
b. Not in the Labor Force	9,262	10,785	11,055	10,922	9,829
c. Employed Persons by Class of Worker	14,985	14,334	14,323	14,588	15,699
1. Wage and Salary Workers	6,863	6,545	6,415	6,419	6,595
(a) In Private Business	5,587	5,302	5,131	5,134	5,275
(b) In Government	1,276	1,242	1,284	1,284	1,321
2. Self-employed	5,560	5,484	5,774	5,887	6,283
3. Unpaid Family Workers	2,513	2,273	2,081	2,249	2,804
4. Class of Worker not Reported	49	33	53	32	17

Source: Quarterly Household Survey, National Cenus and Statistics Office.

These figures show some fluctuation in the level of unemployment, but it increased from 3.8% in the third quarter of 1977 to 6.3% in mid-1978. The government has followed an aggressive policy of exporting labour and the Minister of Labour and Employment stated that in 1980 half a million Filipino workers were employed under contract in 107 countries, mostly in the Middle East. In 1980, 141,197 passports were issued to Filipino citizens for purposes of labour or private employment overseas. This constituted 50% of all passports issued in that year.

Approximately half the labour force is employed in agriculture, forestry and fishing.

Table 80 – Employed persons by major industry group (15 years and over)

	1st quarter 1977			2nd quarter 1978
	Total	Male	Female	Total
('000s)				
Total employed persons	**14,985**	**9,939**	**5,046**	**15,699**
Agriculture, forestry, hunting and fishing	7,046	5,606	1,439	8,054
Mining and quarrying	91	85	6	80
Construction	593	590	3	506
Manufacturing	1,837	950	887	1,756
Electricity, gas, water and sanitary services	72	65	7	51
Commerce	1,851	736	1,115	1,660
Transport, storage and communications	704	674	30	658
Government, community, business and recreational services	1,406	715	691	2,600
Personal services other than domestic	1,261	438	824	NA
Industry not reported	124	81	43	335

Source: Quarterly Survey of Households, National Census and Statistics Office

Because the agricultural economy is diversified into a number of major crops there is less seasonal fluctuation in agricultural employment than in countries which are heavily dependent on one crop such as rice in Thailand where there is a pool of 4–5 million unemployed in the off-season for rice.

Well over half the male labour force is employed in the agricultural, forestry and fishing sector compared with about one quarter of the women. There is more female employment in the manufacturing industries, commerce and services.

Table 81 – Percentage distribution of employed persons by major industry group (15 years and over, 1st quarter 1977)

	('000s) 14,985	9,939	5,046
	%	%	%
Agriculture, forestry, hunting and fishing	47.0	56.4	28.5
Mining and quarrying	0.6	0.8	0.1
Construction	4.0	5.9	0.1
Manufacturing	12.2	9.6	17.6
Electricity, gas, water and sanitary services	0.5	0.6	0.1
Commerce	12.4	7.4	22.1
Transport, storage and communication	4.7	6.8	0.6
Government, community, business and recreational services	9.4	7.2	13.7
Personal services other than domestic	8.4	4.4	16.3
Industry not reported	0.8	0.8	0.8

Source: Quarterly Household Survey, National Census and Statistics Office.

WAGE RATES

Minimum wage legislation exists, which is periodically up-dated. The following table is for daily wage rates actually current in Metro Manila in September 1980, and only one averages below the minimum level set in August 1980; the lowest for Cigar and Cigarette Makers at Pesos 12.73 per day.

Table 82 – Daily money and real wage-rates in industrial establishments in Greater Manila (September 1980)

	Daily Average Wage
Blacksmiths	27.90
Boilermen	22.50
Carpenters	19.64
Drivers	22.17
Cigar and Cigarette Makers	12.73
Compositors	19.16
Electricians	24.58
Foremen	36.40
Lathemen	21.61
Linotypists	22.65
Tinsmiths	23.10
Masons	20.10
Mechanics	29.00
Painters	22.65
Plumbers	18.36
Unskilled labourers	15.92

Source: Central Bank of the Philippines

The following figures are abstracted from a multi-county survey conducted every few years by the Union Bank of Switzerland, and wage rates are shown in occupation categories comparable to those used by the Central Bank of the Philippines. At the lower, skilled-worker end of the scale the rates are comparable in each set of data.

88

Table 83 – Daily wage rates for various occupations Manila (1980)

	Daily wage
Primary school teacher	26.5
Automobile mechanic	25.1
Construction worker	23.7
Toolmaker/lathe operator	32.1
Secretary	44.7
Sales girl	19.5
Textile worker	16.7

Source: Union Bank of Switzerland.

A serious problem facing the Philippines is the decline in living standards during the last decade caused by inflation and the depreciating purchasing power of the peso, which have outstripped wage increases.

Thus in 1980, although skilled labour wages have nearly doubled in relation to 1972, the real wage is two thirds, or 63.2% of what it was in 1972. For unskilled labour the erosion has been even worse, the 1980 real wage being only half or 52.5% of what it was in 1972. There is thus a widening gap between the skilled and unskilled labour living standard, and the government is worried about the possible threat this poses to the stability of the Philippines.

Table 84 – Money and real wage rate increases in Greater Manila (1972=100)

	Money wage rates		Real wage rates	
	Skilled labourers	Unskilled labourers	Skilled labourers	Unskilled labourers
1973	105.3	102.6	92.4	90.0
1974	115.1	110.8	75.6	72.8
1975	119.7	120.1	72.7	72.9
1976	124.4	126.2	71.2	72.3
1977	137.5	132.9	72.9	70.4
1978	154.4	138.4	76.1	68.4
1979	172.3	147.1	67.2	57.4
1980	182.6	151.8	63.2	52.5

(NB: 1979 and 1980 figures are for month of September, previous years' are annual averages.)

Source: Central Bank of the Philippines

The following table demonstrates that wage increases have been very uneven across different occupation groups with construction, mining, agriculture, transport and services, lagging far behind other occupations with higher base rates, and being below the average for all workers in 1979. Thus the widening gap is not only between unskilled and skilled workers, but also between skilled and higher level occupations.

Table 85 – Index of average monthly earnings of salaried employees and wage earners by industry in the Philippines (1972=100)
June 1979

	Salaried employees	Wage earners
All workers	227.5	195.4
Agriculture	215.1	165.9
Mining and quarrying	190.8	343.9
Manufacturing	200.3	196.4
Electricity, gas and water	336.7	130.1
Construction	190.2	243.5
Wholesale & retail trade	247.7	164.6
Transport, storage & communication	197.8	293.2
Finance, insurance, real estate and business services	337.4	256.0
Community, social & personal services	177.6	166.2

Source: Central Bank of the Philippines

It was against this growing disparity of earning power, and a problem of real and growing poverty, that the government has set minimum wage rates, which were most recently up-graded in August 1980, in most cases by one peso a day.

Table 86 – Minimum wage rates set on August 18, 1980

Non-agricultural workers

    Metro Manila   Pesos 14 a day
    Outside Manila   Pesos 13

Agricultural workers

    Plantation   Pesos 11
    Non-plantation   Pesos 10

Cottage industry workers   Pesos 11-13
    (depending on location
    and size of firm)

Source: Ministry of Labour and Employment

LABOUR RELATIONS

The Ministry of Labour and Employment has responsibility for implementing labour policies, and has jurisdiction over labour disputes, with the responsibility of promoting their resolution.

Trades Unions are not yet strongly established in the Philippines, but there are signs of increasing activity. There was some fairly strong industrial union activity prior to the declaration of martial law, but since then it has declined.

Under the Philippine Labour Code of 1974 all employees except those in managerial jobs, and those in non-profit making organisations, have the right to organise themselves into, or to join unions. The closed shop system exists.

The Ministry of Labour and Employment directed the Institute of Labour and Manpower Studies in 1980 to conduct a study of foreign assistance to local trade unions, and itself monitors the activity of foreign labour organisations in the Philippines. The Ministry has developed an early warning system in co-ordination with the military authorities to give notice of unrest in volatile areas.

LABOUR REGULATIONS

There are comprehensive regulations for the employment of labour outlined in the 1974 Labour Code. In addition to minimum wages and the workers' right to organise unions and bargain collectively the Labour Code set the following conditions of work.

* Medicare, including medical and dental care and maternity leave
* Leave entitlements
* Hours worked, with statutory overtime rates of pay
* Public holidays
* Termination of employment
* Social security
* Workmen's compensation in the case of industrial accidents

The hiring of labour for employment overseas must be arranged through a relevant government department such as the Overseas Employment Development Board or the National Seamen's Board.

12 Media and Advertising

MEDIA USAGE

There are three major sources of information on media audiences in the Philippines.

* Media Pulse Inc operates a television audience measurement survey providing monthly TV ratings based on data obtained from 300 television meters installed in a panel of houses in Manila.

* Consumer Pulse Inc offer a Media Index survey report giving audience data for all media. The format of this report is similar to the Media Index which is operated regularly by the Survey Research Group in five other countries and is the established source of media audience data for the industry in all the other countries. The Philippine Media Index is not however conducted regularly.

* PMCRS (Philippine Mass Communications Research Society) operate a survey measuring Print Media audiences, the PMCRS Print Media Exposure Survey. PMCRS also conduct other media surveys on an ad hoc basis.

In addition the Audit Council for Media (ACM) officially audits print media circulation, has been operating for ten years, and has a membership of 71 publications. The ACM publishes the booklet 'Media Information Factbook 1979-80' which will be up-dated in 1982.

Television started in the Philippines with the operational launch of IBC in 1958 in Manila, thus following closely behind the first television broadcasting in Asia, which started in Thailand in 1955. Since then four other networks have started operations in Manila, the most recent being CNDE - GTV in 1978. All of the five stations operate in other locations, and GMA, Radio Philippines and IBC have steadily extended their range of coverage over the Philippines.

The stations are frequently referred to by their channel number in Manila, but they operate under different channel designations in other cities.

All the networks have originating stations in Manila, and cover the rest of the country with replay stations; which can replay original transmission from Manila or originate their own broadcasts; relay stations which cannot originate but can relay either from the originating or the replay station; translator stations which transmit signals from any of the other three types of stations, within a defined area.

The Research and Statistics Section of the National Telecommunications Commission recorded an increase from 22 licensed television broadcasting stations in 1974 to 31 in mid-1979, operated within the five networks.

The five television networks are:

CNDE - GTV	-	Manila Channel 4, 2 other areas
GMA Radio-Television Arts	-	Manila Channel 7, 18 other areas
Radio Philippines Network	-	Manila Channel 9, 16 other areas
IBC	-	Manila Channel 13, 9 other areas
BBC (Banahaw Broadcasting Corp)	-	Manila Channel 2, 2 other areas

There are two other local broadcasting stations in the south; Southern Broadcasting Network in Davao City, and Zamboanga Television Corporation in Zamboanga City. Both of these stations operate as part of the Radio Philippines Network. SBN in Davao also operates a radio station.

There is some variation in the figures for incidence of television ownership in the Philippines, but over the last decade the recorded figures show a trend of growth. The increase in the level of set ownership has been faster in the rural areas of the country, but the incidence outside towns is still extremely low. In 1980 a census of 239,372 households in Metro Manila, conducted by Media Pulse Inc, established a set ownership level of 60%, which was considerably lower than previous sample survey figures.

Table 87 – Television set ownership;
1975 and 1979 by urban/rural

	Urban		Rural	
	1975	1979	1975	1979
	%	%	%	%
Own a television set	42	47	3	7

Source: Consumer Pulse Inc.

Rural coverage is considerably higher in Luzon (13%) than in the south (3% in the Visayas and 2% in Mindanao).

Audience data is confined to urban areas, and the PUMS data shows that about two thirds of all adults aged 12 and over watched television weekly in the main area, Manila.

Table 88 – Television viewing by region (urban)

	Greater Manila	Luzon N	Luzon C/S	Bicol	Visayas C/E	Visayas W	Mindanao
	%	%	%·	%	%	%	%
% of adults (12+) who live in a TV home	70	34	40	10	25	23	28
% of adults (12+) who viewed in past week	67	33	39	7	24	22	25

Source: Pulse Urban Market Study 1979

Radio is a medium with much wider spread of coverage in the Philippines, both in terms of broadcasting stations and ownership of sets. In mid-1978 the Research and Statistics Section of the National Telecommunications Commission recorded 239 licensed AM Radio Broadcasting stations and 34 FM. The growth shown is from 106 AM and 20 FM stations in 1974.   These stations broadcast 229 radio channels.

Radio broadcasts are transmitted mainly in Tagalog, English and a wide range of regional languages, although there are some stations which transmit only in one local dialect.

Radio penetration is growing, and the main growth is in the rural areas as they catch up with the already well covered urban areas. There is better agreement in the statistical data on radio ownership, and the following table corresponds closely with the several other published sources.

Table 89 – Radio ownership;
1975 and 1979, Manila/Urban/Rural

	Metro Manila		Urban		Rural	
	1975	1979	1975	1979	1975	1979
	%	%	%	%	%	%
Own a radio set	79	85	72	77	54	63

Source: Consumer Pulse Inc.

The incidence of radio listening is lower than the incidence of set ownership, and the gap tends to be higher where television penetration is higher.

Table 90 – Radio listening by region (urban)

	Greater Manila	N	Luzon C/S	Bicol	C/E	Visayas W	Mindanao
	%	%	%	%	%	%	%
% of adults (12+) who live in a home with radio	85	82	72	72	76	68	76
% of adults (12+) who listened in past week	72	74	61	67	70	59	67

Source: Pulse Urban Market Study 1979

Despite the fairly high penetration of radio in the Philippines, media planning becomes extremely complex in view of the large number of local stations scattered throughout the country. The Kapisanan ng mga Brodkaster sa Pilipinas (Association of Broadcasters in the Philippines) had 81 member networks in 1976. By 1979 this had increased to 91, all of whom except one are radio broadcasters, and 81 are commercial.

Newspapers enjoy a penetration level in Manila similar to other major capitals in the region, but even in urban areas of the Philippines everyday readership drops sharply outside Manila.

Table 91 – Newspaper reading by region (urban)

	Greater Manila	Luzon N	C/S	Bicol	Visayas C/S	W	Mindanao
	%	%	%	%	%	%	%
% of adults (12+) who read a newspaper every day	67	35	30	23	39	27	37

(N.B. The daily frequency has been derived by calibrating weekly recency by numbers read per week)

Source: Pulse Urban Market Study 1979

This makes an interesting comparison with Thailand, which has a comparable literacy level, and where newspaper readership in the urban areas outside Bangkok is as high or even in some cases higher than in the capital, as is radio listening.

The Philippines had a long tradition of a dynamic daily press, which thrived on the sensationalism of pre-martial law politics. This is less the case in recent years, but it remains an important medium.

The major newspaper is Bulletin Today, which has an audited circulation of about 300,000 for both the Sunday and daily editions. Two other English language newspapers, Daily Express and Times Journal have circulations of 120,000 and 80,000. The fourth major circulation newspaper in the Philippines is Balita, a Tagalog/Pilipino language publication. Circulation of these four leading newspapers is concentrated in Manila.

Magazine penetration presents quite a different picture from newspaper usage. Readership figures are nearly as high in urban areas in the provinces as they are in Manila.

Table 92 - Magazine reading by region (urban)

	Greater Manila	N	Luzon C/S	Bicol	Visayas C/E	W	Mindanao
	%	%	%	%	%	%	%
% of adults (12+) who read a magazine in past month	66	67	54	55	70	51	59

Source: Pulse Urban Market Study 1979

It may be that the frequency of issue of newspapers is a factor inhibiting their use in the provinces, a factor which does not affect weekly, fortnightly or monthly magazines.

There are over 60 major magazines published in the Philippines, the leading five being in Tagalog English. All the press is fairly regional in its circulation, exemplified in the two publications in positions 6 and 7, which are in Cebuano and Ilocano.

Liwayway   -   Circulation c. 140,000 - Tagalog
                 - short stories, social news stories

Kislap   -   Circulation c. 100,000 - Tagalog
               - movie stories

Mod Filipina -   Circulation c. 90,000 - English
                  - fashion

Women's journal - Circulation c. 80,000 - English

Women's Home - Circulation c. 70,000 - English

Bisaya   -   Circulation c. 60,000 - Cebuano
               - stories, serials, news

Bannawag -   Circulation c. 40,000 - Ilocano
               - stories, serials, news

Magazines are stronger in rural areas than daily newspapers, and relatively stronger among women and younger people.

Comics are an unusual feature of the Philippine media mix. There are approximately 50. They are weekly publications and all are in Pilipino/Tagalog.

They enjoy high circulation, and the top 10 are well above the circulation figures for magazines.

In 1979 eight comics had circulation figures ranging from 100,000 up to 150,000. The top ten comics are:

        Pilipino Komics
        Aliwan Komics
        Tagalog Klasics
        Hiwaga Komics
        Espesyal Komics
        Superstar Komics
        Love Story Illustrated
        Darna Komics
        Bondying Movie Special
        Pinoy Komics

Note that even those with English language titles are still printed in Pilipino/Tagalog.

Readership of comics is approximately the same as magazines in Manila, and in most of the provincial urban areas slightly higher.

Table 93 - Comic reading by region (urban)

	Greater Manila	N	Luzon C/S	Bicol	Visayas C/E	W	Mindanao
	%	%	%	%	%	%	%
% of adults (12+) who read a comic in past week	61	70	72	72	55	64	62

Source: Pulse Urban Market Study 1979

The following table shows clearly the difference in audience profile between the three print media. Newspapers are fairly evenly read across all socio-economic classes in Greater Manila, with a slight up-market bias. Magazines are very much up-market, comics the reverse.

Table 94 - Newspaper/magazine/comic reading by socio-economic class (Greater Manila)

	AB	C	D	E
	%	%	%	%
% of adults (12+) who read:				
newspaper in past week	96	97	85	81
magazine in past month	91	82	61	43
comic in past week	30	55	66	72

Source: Pulse Urban Market Study 1979

(The point should be made that this data refers to Greater Manila only).

In terms of age newspapers are very evenly read across all age groups, but there is a slight leaning towards younger readers for magazines.

The table also demonstrates the nature of the readership of comics, which may be a surprise to anyone unfamiliar with the Philippines. Although readership of comics is higher among the under 30s, about half the over 30s are regular weekly readers of comics.

Table 95 – Newspaper/magazine/comic reading by age (Greater Manila)

	12-19	20-29	30-39	40
	%	%	%	%
% of adults (12+) who read:				
newspaper in past week	87	89	90	85
magazine in past month	71	69	62	60
comic in past week	65	68	56	45

Source: Pulse Urban Market Study 1979

Given these large readership and circulation figures it is surprising that to date comics do not attract a great deal of advertising revenue.

Cinema is a more popular medium in the Philippines than in any neighbouring countries, and approximately 80% of the adult population go to the cinema at some time.

Table 96 – Cinema going by region (urban)

	Greater Manila	Luzon N	Luzon B/S	Bicol	Visayas C/E	Visayas W	Mindanao
	%	%	%	%	%	%	%
% of adults (12+) who ever visit a cinema	86	76	79	88	83	70	81

Source: Pulse Urban Market Study 1979

Frequency is exceptionally high: in Greater Manila 51% of adults visited the cinema in the past month, compared with 34% nationally.

There are over 75 cinemas in Greater Manila, over 45 in the two major cities of Cebu and Davao, and over 650 in the rest of the country.

The cinemas in the three major cities average 6 screenings a day, and in the smaller towns 3 to 4.

ADVERTISING RATES

There is wide variation across media and within media in both advertising rates and cost per thousand. This variation is magnified by the scale of discounting for multiple insertions. The following figures are a very rough indication of scale in early 1980, for single black and white insertions in the local print media, with a few on either side of these figures.

Provincial weeklies	Pesos 900-1,300
Magazines	Pesos 1,500-3,000
Comics (top 10)	Pesos 800-1,300

The cost of radio spots range in several categories in Metro Manila:

Manila Radio	30 sec	Pesos 20-50, 50-150
	60 sec	Pesos 20-50, 100-250
Provin Radio	30 sec	Pesos 5-10
	60 secs	Pesos 5-20

Television is complex because it is possible to book part spots, single spots, breakspots and programme sponsorships, and costs range from Pesos 50 for breakspots in limited areas to Pesos 5,000 for full network spots.

Cinema rates are more even, ranging from Pesos 200-500 per day of 6-7 screenings in Manila; Pesos 70-120 per day in Cebu and Davao; Pesos 45-75 per day in other provincial cinemas, with 3-4 screenings a day.

ADVERTISING RESTRICTIONS

Television commercials have to be approved by the Philippine Board of Advertising before being screened.

Print media advertising needs no prior approval, it is self regulating. However, the Philippine Board of Advertising can and does ban advertisements after they appear in publications.

ADVERTISING AGENCIES

The following is the list of advertising agencies who were members of the 4As (Association of Accredited Advertising Agencies (Philippines)) in 1979.

A Sison & Associates
Able Advertising
Ace-Compton Advertising Inc
Adformatix Inc
Admakers Inc
Adtrade Inc
Adver Inc
Advertising and Marketing Associates Inc
Asia Communications Centre
Aspect Communications Inc
Associated Media
Atlas Promotions and Marketing
Avellana & Associates
Cathprom Advertising Co
Creative Concepts
Commerce Advertising Corporation
Communications Associates of Asia Inc
Convey Advertising
General Ads Inc
Grant Advertising (Phils.) Inc
Great Wall Advertising
Hemisphere
R.K. Davis & Associates

International Advertising

J Romero & Associates

J Walter Thompson Co (Phils.) Inc

Link Advertising

Manprom Advertising Agency

Markom Advertising Associates

Marketing & Advertising Counsel

MKTG & ADVTG Resources Corp (Marc)

McCann Erickson (Phils.) Inc

Pacifica Publicity Bureau

Peace Advertising

Phil. Advertising Counselors Inc.

Philprom Inc

Project General Ads

Reach Advertising Inc

The Marketing Communications Group Inc

The Motivators Inc

The Word Associates Inc

Viewpoint Advertising

Well Advertising & Marketing Agency

Yabut & Associates

The Philippines has one of the lowest per capita advertising expenditures in Asia.

Table 97 – Advertising expenditure in the countries of Asia Pacific (1978)

	Total annual expenditure (US$ million)	Expenditure per head of population (US$)
Japan	5,604	49.1
Australia	1,145	81.2
South Korea	277	7.6
Hong Kong	95	20.7
New Zealand	91	28.3
Thailand	86	1.9
Taiwan	86	5.0
Philippines	77	1.7
Indonesia	57	.4
Malaysia	55	4.4
Singapore	51	21.9

Source: Survey Research Singapore (Pte) Ltd.

13 Retail Trade

The wholesale and retail trade is an important constituent of the economy and has been growing at an above average rate over the last decade. In 1972 it accounted for 12.6% of GDP, in 1979 15.6%. This is on a par with Thailand, at 16.5%.

Table 98 - Gross Value Added and Implicit Price Index of Wholesale and Retail Trade, and other industries

	GVA (Current prices in million pesos)	Implicit Price Index - Dec 1979 (1972 = 100)
Manufacturing	52,798	249.7
Agriculture, fisheries and forestry	52,582	232.8
Wholesale and retail trade	33,911	300.2
Hotels and restaurants	2,647	194.2
Services (exc hotels and restaurants)	20,498	209.5
Construction	15,931	250.2
Transport and communication	14,244	317.2

Source: National Economic and Development Authority

Relative to 1972, by the end of 1979 the wholesale and retail trade sector had a higher Implicit Price Index at 300.2 than any other sector of the Philippine economy.

The Philippines is amply supplied with data about the retail trade, having the longest established retail audit panel service in South east Asia, which is operated by Dealer Pulse Inc. Dealer Pulse conducted the first census of stores in greater Manila in 1972, and has repeated the census every four years, the most recent being in November 1980.

In 1975 the National Census and Statistics Office listed 348,281 wholesale and retail establishments throughout the Philippines.

The 1980 store census conducted by Dealer Pulse counted 43,138 outlets in Greater Manila, with a further 4,192 in Bulacan and Rizal. The most numerous category is the 'sari-sari', a type of small general store, which constitutes over half the total number of outlets with 24,425 in Greater Manila and a further 2,299 in Bulacan and Rizal. This is the largest retail outlet category throughout the Philippines. Supermarkets are increasing in number, and in 1980 there were 76 in Greater Manila. Manila has still to grow a long way with this type of outlet to reach the levels of Singapore which has nearly 500, for a population less than half the size. A feature of Manila supermarkets is that some of them rival the huge hyper-markets of France in size.

The following list is derived from the definitions and criteria used by Dealer Pulse in classifying retail outlets. The full list of definitions is more comprehensive, and contains further classification details for analysis purposes which are hardly relevant in this volume. Dealer Pulse defines a retail outlet as a commercial establishment which sells at least 75% of its goods direct to the consumer, and classifies them as follows:

1. Supermarket - This is a large retail store which sells various commodities including food, household wares, and personal items arranged in sections. The distinguishing features of a supermarket are:

   a. It is usually air-conditioned.

   b. It has a restaurant or snack counter sharing the same entrance as the store itself.

   c. It has at least three check-out counters with cash registers.

   d. It is self-service. Pushcarts or baskets are provided to customers for the goods they pick from open shelves.

   e. At least 20% of the display area is devoted to non-food items.

2. Grocery Store - This is smaller than a supermarket but it sells generally the same line of products. Compared to a supermarket, a grocery store sells more edible (food) items relative to other product lines. As in a super-

market, the customers have access to the products. One prominent characteristic of a grocery store which is not generally found in a sari-sari store is the presence of a cash register. Also, it has 1 or 2 check-out counters.

3. <u>Sari-Sari Store</u> - This is a small store selling a wide variety of food and non-food packaged/manufactured items by the piece, and often by the lowest possible quantity (tingi). The distinguishing features are:

   a. It does not issue receipts to customers.

   b. It does not allow customers to pick things they want to buy as goods in display or in open shelves are beyond their reach.

   c. It usually sells repacked items: e.g. the owner breaks up manufacturer's items into smaller units like dip-out kerosene, cooking oil, powdered detergents, sugar, etc.

Stores that are selling <u>only</u> non-packaged food items such as rice and other cereals, fresh vegetables, fish and meat are not considered as sari-sari stores according to our definition. Therefore, they are not included in the store listing.

Sari-Sari stores are sub-classified into "A", "B" and tienda. A sari-sari store that has any of the following characteristics is classified as "A":

   a. It has a cash register/adding machine/or desk type calculator.

   b. Total inventory of canned and bottled goods on display (excluding soft drinks) is at least 400 pieces.

   c. The average daily sales is at least P450.

Sari-Sari stores that do not have any of the above characteristics are classified as "B". Generally sari-sari "B"s have an inventory of 100 to 399 canned and bottled goods (excluding soft drinks).

A tienda is a small sari-sari store that has less than 100 units of canned and bottled goods on display.

4. <u>Market Stall</u> - This is a sari-sari store inside a market building.

5. <u>Drugstores</u> - An establishment primarily engaged in the retail sale of preparation drugs and medicines, toiletries, and novelty items.

Drugstores are sub-classified into chain and independent.

6. <u>Department Store</u> - This is a store engaged in the retail sale of various non-food product lines such as ready-made clothing, shoes, cosmetics, men's wear, household appliances and furnishings, luggage. These lines are normally arranged in separate departments with each department having its own personnel accountable for sales.

7. <u>Bazaar</u> - This is smaller than a department store. It carries more than one line of non-food items such as household wares, personal care items, cosmetics, kitchen utensils, etc.

8. <u>Gift Shop/Cosmetic Store</u> - A store primarily engaged in the retail sale of gift and novelty items such as dolls, piggy banks, albums and picture frames. A cosmetic store is one primarily engaged in the retail sale of cosmetics and toilet articles.

9. <u>Hardware</u> - A store engaged primarily in the sale of construction tools and supplies, and articles made of metal. It may carry related lines such as insecticides and household wax.

10. <u>School/Institutional Canteen</u> - An outlet for meals, snacks, and refreshments exclusively at the service of students and employees of a particular school or institution such as hospitals, offices, and factories. It is located within the premises of the school or institution.

11. <u>Refreshment Parlor</u> - An outlet for merienda items (sandwiches, mami, siopao, spaghetti, palabok, etc.) and beverages (soft drinks, coffee, tea). It does not serve heavy or full meals.

12. Restaurant - A large outlet for meals and snacks where food is usually ordered and served. Meals are usually cooked as ordered but may also be pre-cooked.

13. Carinderia - A small outlet for meals and snacks. Food is usually pre-cooked and it is usually self-service (turo-turo).

114. Terminal Stalls - Stores found within the premises of bus terminals. They are similar to sari-sari stores in appearance except that their main line of business is not canned goods but biscuits, candies, snack foods, refreshments, and "pasalubong" items which are usually native specialities of the locality.

15. Bakery/Bake Shops - A store that sells a wide variety of baked items such as bread, mamon, ensaymada, including cakes and pastries and other oven-cooked items.

16. Gas Stations - An establishment engaged primarily in the retail of automotive fuel and other related products as gear oil and filters, and accessories. It often offers automotive and maintenance services. It may also sell insecticides and household wax.

17. Candy Factory - An establishment engaged primarily in the manufacture of confectionery products.

18. Hotels - An establishment that provides lodging and often food for travellers. Motels and inns are also considered as hotels. Boarding houses are not considered as hotels.

19. Beauty Parlors - An establishment engaged in a wide variety of grooming services for women. Most common are hairstyling, manicure, and make-ups. A beauty parlor may also be unisex.

20. Funeral Parlor - An establishment that attends to the needs of the dead, from embalment to burial. It usually has one or more chapels.

21. <u>Ice Cream/Ice Drop Factory</u> - An establishment engaged in the manufacture of frozen cream-based products. "Ice buko" factories are included.

22. <u>Wine/Liquor Shop</u> - A store primarily engaged in the sale of wines and spirits and other intoxicating drinks.

14 Information Sources

For a comprehensive listing of over 75 statistical and economic sources of information on the Philippines, the reader is referred to 'Sources of Asian Pacific Economic Information' by Blauvelt and Durlacher (Gower Publishing Company Limited - London). In 1981 'Sources of Asian Pacific Marketing Information' will be published, by the same co-authors and publisher.

Below are some key publications:

PHILIPPINES

Images from the Future: The Philipines in the Year 2000	Population Centre Foundation
Philippine Statistical Yearbook	National Economic and Development Authority
Five-Year Philippine Development Plan, 1978-1982	"
Philippine Development (monthly)	"
1980 Philippine Development Report	"
Philippine Economic Indicators	"
Media Information Philippines	Audit Council for Media
Philippine Factbook	Pulse Group of Companies
Fookien Times Yearbook	Fookien Times
Kapisanan ng mga Brodcaster sa Pilipina	Association of Broadcasters in the Philippines
Doing Business in the Philippines	Price Waterhouse, Joaquin Cunanan & Co
Doing Business in the Philippines	SGV & Co
Investment Opportunities in the Philippines	Board of Investments
13th Investment Priorities Plan	"

3rd Agricultural Investment
Priorities Plan   "

11th Export Priorities Plan   "

Questions and Answers on Foreign
Investment in the Philippines   "

Ministry of Industry '77 and '78   "

Export Bulletin (Quarterly)   "

Non-traditional Exports   "

1979 Annual Report   "

Philippine Industry and Investment
(Quarterly)   "

PHILIPPINE ADDRESSES

Association of Broadcasters of
the Philippines
Suite 402
4th Floor, Chateau Makati Building
F. Zobal Street
Makati
Rizal

tel 86-64-51

Board of Investments
Industry & Investment Building
Buenida Avenue Extension
Makati
Metro Manila

PO Box 676 Makati or PO Box 181 Greenhills

Cable INVESTBORO

Bureau of Foreign Trade
Department of Trade
Arcadia Building
Quezon Boulevard Extension
Quezon City

Bureau of National and Foreign Information
Department of Public Information
Beneficial Life Building
Solana
Intamuros
Metro Manila

Business Day Corporation
113 West Avenue
Quezon City

tel 99-15-46

Chamber of Commerce of the Philippines
Magallanes Drive
Manila 2801

tel 49-83-21

National Census and Statistics Office
PO Box 779
Metro Manila

National Economic and Development Authority
NEDA Quezon City Complex
E. de los Santos Avenue
Dilinan
Metro Manila

Private Development Corporation of the Philippines
PDCP Building
Ayala Avenue
Makati
Metro Manila

15 Market Research

RESEARCH FACILITIES

A wide range of established research services is available in the Philippines, including the largest established retail audit in Southeast Asia, and the first Asian developed television meter system outside Japan. Standards vary from excellent to questionable, and it is probably the most price sensitive market in Asia Pacific.

Unlike the other Asian countries except for Malaysia, research is well developed with rural coverage, partly because of interest in social research in the early years that the industry was established.

Both quantitative and qualitative facilities are available, with many techniques in common use. There is a wide range of consumer, retail and media syndicated research reports available for purchase, nearly all from one company, which in some cases offer trend data over 5 or more years.

Fieldwork can be commissioned by itself, and there are small companies offering only this service.

Telephone surveys are so far in their infancy, partly because of the poor telephone system, and partly because of the comparatively low cost of personal interviewing.

Postal interviewing is also uncommon.

Interviewing is conducted in several vernacular languages and English.

Industrial research has been carried out for some years. There are a number of directories of larger organisations for sampling purposes.

There is a highly developed syndicated retail audit capability.

Average costs are as follows:

a)   Probability sample of 1,000 housewives - Pesos 60,000
30 minute questionnaire - 150 tables and diagnostic report

b)   Four group discussions with sample comprising 20% of
total adult population including a diagnostic report Pesos 15,000

c)   200 product test personal interviews - one call - 50 tables and
diagnostic report Pesos 20,000

MARKET RESEARCH COMPANIES

Asia Research Organisation Inc
ABC Compound
2251 Pasong Tamo
Makati
Metro Manila

tel 879791
telex 23075

Consumer Pulse Inc
Pulse Building
6 San Rafael Street
Barrio Kapitolyo
Pasig
Metro Manila

tel 69-38-705
cable Conpulse, Pasig

telex 64505 ETP PSG PN Attn: Consumer Pulse

Dealer Pulse Inc
Pulse Building
6 San Rafael Street
Barrio Kapitolyo
Pasig
Metro Manila

tel 69-38-705
telex 64505 ETP PSG PN Attn: Dealer Pulse

Media Pulse Inc
Pulse Building
6 San Rafael Street
Barrio Kapitolyo
Pasig
Metro Manila

tel 69-38-705
telex 64505 ETP PSG PN Attn: Media Pulse

SGV & Co
SGV Building
6760 Ayala Avenue
Makati
Metro Manila

tel 89-30-11
telex   RCA 22160
         ITT 5096
         EE 63743

AVAILABLE RESEARCH REPORTS

The **Pulse Group of Companies** is the main supplier of syndicated research reports, with five services offering reports on over 140 products. Some of these services offer trend data for several years on a selection of products. The following is the list of reports available in mid-1981. Further details and prices can be obtained from any **SRG** office or from **The Asia Pacific Centre.** Brand data is available in all of these reports, except for media audience analysis.

TV RATING REPORT

Monthly television audience rating reports, based on a television meter panel in Manila, are available from Media Pulse.

PULSE URBAN MARKET STUDY (PUMS)

A quarterly survey of 2,700 households in urban areas of the Philippines. In addition to published product reports, omnibus facilities are available for clients to add their own questions. Reports are available for the following products:

BEVERAGES/FOOD PRODUCTS

Biscuits, Bread-fillings, Breakfast Cereals, Coffee, Canned Meat, Powdered Milk, Tea, Desserts/Gelatin, Fruit-flavoured Drinks, Fresh Milk.

TOILETRIES

Absorbent Cotton, Cleansing Cream, Cotton Buds, Rubbing Alcohol, Sanitary Napkins, Shampoo, Skin/Body Lotion, Toilet Soap, Sunscreen Lotion, Suntan Lotion, Talcum Powder, Toothbrushes, Creme Rinse Conditioner, Deodorant/Anti-Perspirant, Dental Floss, Hair Grooming, Hair Spray, Men's Hair-dressings, Personal Care Products.

HOUSEHOLD PRODUCTS

Adhesive Tapes, Analgesics, Anthelmentics, Antiseptics, Baby Cologne, Baby Oil, Baby Powder, Chewing Gum, Chocolates, Cleaner/Disinfectant, Cooking Oil, Roach Baits, Shoe Polish, Toilet Bowl Cleaner, Vitamins, Cotylenol, Diaper Liners, Disposable Wipes, Floor Wax, Furniture Care Products, Gauze, Home-Care, Insect-icides, Detergent, Medicated Plasters, Nursing Pads.

MISCELLANEOUS

Cameras, Cigarettes, Plastic Strips, Jeans, Paperback Books.

MEDIA INDEX SERVICE

Reports are avilable from 1978 and 1979 rounds of PUMS providing comprehensive audience analysis for television, radio, cinema, newspapers and magazines.

GREATER MANILA RETAIL PANEL (GMRP)

Monthly retail audit reports are available containing the following information:

- Retail sales and brand share of sales
- Stock cover
- Distribution and out-of-stock levels
- Average buying and selling prices

The following products are covered:

Adhesive Bandages, Bag Soups, Disposable Ballpens, Bleach, Cheese, Chocolate Drinks, Cleanser, Coffee, Cologne, Condiments, Confectionery, Corn Starch, Diapers/Diaper Liners, Feminine Hygiene, Noodles/Cube Soups, Iodised Salt/Mustard/Vinegar, Jellies, Non-refrigerated Margarine, Refrigerated Margarine, Milk, Mouthwash, Paper Products, Pasta, Peanut Butter, Pickles, Sandwich Spreads/Salad Dressing/Mayonnaise, Scrubbing Pads, Liquid Seasoning, Shampoo, Talcum/Baby Powder, Oil, Lotion, Anthelmentics, Contraceptives, Corn Curls, Corned Beef, Deodorant, Eye Wash, Household Wax, Laundry Products, Oats, Razors/Razor Blades, Toilet Soap, Vienna Sausage, Cereals, Mentholated Candies, Ham, Bacon, Hot Dogs, Infant Milk, Air Freshener, Conditioners, Toothbrushes, Toothpaste.

PULSE NATIONAL RETAIL INDEX

Reports similar to those in the GMRP are available for the whole of the Philippines, with data starting in 1979, for the following products:

Adhesive Bandages, Air Fresheners, Agri-Chemicals, Analgesics, Baby Oil, Cereals, Cheese, Confectionery, Conditioners, Corned Beef, Cleansers, Colognes, Cotton Balls, Disinfectants, Feeding Bottles, Floor Care, Fruit Juices/Concentrates, Insecticide, Infant Milk Food, Laundry Products, Lotion, Milk, Oil, Paper Products, Pasta, Pickles, Mayonnaise, Sandwich Spread, Sanitary Napkins, Snack Foods, Shampoo, Toilet Soap, Toothbrushes, Toothpaste, Talcum/Baby Powder.

URBAN PHILIPPINE RETAIL PANEL

Similar reports, with urban coverage of the whole of the Philippines are available for:

Chewing Gum, Cologne, Cotton Buds, Household Wax, Insecticides, Lotion, Milk, Sanitary Napkins, Shampoo, Talcum Powder.

ANNUAL COMMERCIAL BANK STUDIES

Published by SGV, there are 9 reports, one for each ASEAN country (including the Philippines). The Philippines report has quarterly updates.

ASIAN PROFILES

A major media and marketing survey of upper-class men covering eight capital cities in Southeast and East Asia including Manila. The survey was carried out by SRG companies on behalf of Time, Newsweek International and Readers' Digest Association Far East Limited, from any of whom information can be obtained.

Notes for the tables

- A 'household' is defined as a group of people who sleep under the same roof and normally eat together.

- An 'adult' is a person aged 15 years or over.

- Household expenditure is the total monthly expenditure in the household as estimated by the survey respondent.

- Population estimates are those applicable at the time of the survey.

- Percentages have been rounded and may not always add to 100% precisely.

- An asterisk in the body of a table means less than one half per cent. A blank space or dash means zero.

- An asterisk beside a year means the figures are preliminary for the year.

- The letters N.A. mean not available for this publication.

- The letters nec mean not elsewhere classified.

Index

Abaca, 73,79

Absorbent cotton, 116

Adhesive tape, 116-118

Advertising expenditure, 103

Advertising rates, 101

Advertising restrictions, 102

Age distribution, 11

Agri-chemicals, 118

Agricultural Investment Incentives
Act, 57,58,60-62

Agriculture, 72

Agro-industries, 60

Air conditioners, 40

Aircraft imports, 82

Air freshener, 117,118

Aliwan Kounics, 98

Alcohol products, 61

Analgesics, 116,118

Animal feed, 62,63

Animal oils & fats imports, 82

Anthelmentics, 116,117

Antiseptics, 116

Asia Research Organisation Inc, 114

Asian Profiles, 119

Assistance Team for Foreign
Investment (ATFI), 69-71

Assets of financial institutions, 51

Association of Broadcasters of
the Philippines, 96,111

Audit Council for Media (ACM), 92

Aviation development, 47

Baby cologne, 30,116

Baby freshener, 30

Baby lotion, 29

Baby oil, 30,116-118

Baby powder, 116,117